The
Incredible
Reality
of
You

THE
INCREDIBLE
REALITY
OF
YOU

A Spiritual Guide to the Awakening of Consciousness

AWAKENING WORLD PUBLISHING
VANCOUVER ISLAND, BC, CANADA

Author: Lawrence (lorn) Hoff

Co-Author/Editor: Lucia Hoff

Cover Design by lorn

First Edition, June 2019

Library and Archives Canada

The Incredible Reality of YOU / LUCIALORN

ISBN: 978-1-7753359-0-0

Published in Canada by:

Awakening World Publishing

PO 373 Chemainus, BC

Canada V0R 1K0

www.awakeningworld.net

DEDICATED TO ALL SEEKERS OF TRUTH

You hold in your hands the key to the true awakening to the ultimate reality of your existence, and to the continued unfoldment of Consciousness.

Journey into Truth as you read about the stages and states of Consciousness and open to deeper realities of your Self and the universe on the path to total Awakening.

May this book be a guiding light on your journey into

the Incredible Reality of You.

CONTENTS

THE
INCREDIBLE
REALITY
OF
YOU

PREFACE

If you are not interested in expanding your consciousness to its limits, and beyond, or in knowing the real truth about your existence, then this is not the book for you. If you are interested in awakening to reality as it actually is, gaining a deeper appreciation of subtle levels of creation, deepening your knowledge and experience of the total range of consciousness, and experiencing real freedom, peace and joy, then read on.

This book is about Reality as it really is, not the way it appears through the senses or is understood by the mind. It is about awakening to the true reality of who and what you are beyond your mind and senses, beyond all labels and conditioning, beyond all concepts and beliefs, and beyond your wildest imaginations.

This Awakening does not happen through your mind, intellect or emotions. It happens within the innermost core of your being: to the sense of "I am, I exist". It is the same sense of Being and existing you are experiencing now, only not entangled with your thoughts, sensations, emotions or perceptions. On its own level, beyond the mind, your real inner Self is unlocalized, unbounded and universal.

This book is written to that innermost universal sense of pure Being, not to your mind. It provides the knowledge of the states of Consciousness on the path to total Awakening. Awakening to the true, boundless reality of your inner self is called Self-Realization, and awakening to the true reality of the world and universe is called Enlightenment. This book is about Self-Realization and Enlightenment.

Though much has been written about it by seers throughout the ages, Enlightenment cannot be described in words. It can only be awakened within the innermost core of your Being. For this reason, this book is geared to a gradual buildup and deepening of experience rather than an emphasis on the accumulation of knowledge or information.

You can gain great benefit from this book without understanding any of it. It is not written to your mind, but to your very soul.

If you can stay simple, innocent and open while reading this, something somewhere deep within will resonate with these words and open you to a deeper sense of truth and reality than could ever have been conveyed through words and their meanings.

We have been living only a partial experience of life, conditioned by the seemingly real appearance of the obvious, but asleep to the deeper universal realities of our existence and to what our life here on earth is all about.

This book provides the knowledge of the full range of human consciousness. It begins by bringing to light a few scientific truths to show that the world is not the way it appears to be from the perspective of the mind and senses. It then progressively opens you to a clear understanding of the stages and states of Consciousness on the path to total Awakening.

Throughout the book, there are exercises that take you step by step into the direct experience of expanded levels of consciousness. These are not typical mental exercises. They are designed to stimulate the remembrance of unbounded Awareness within the innermost core of your being. They help to bring your conscious awareness to deeper levels of the experience of its true boundless reality, offering opportunities for true Awakening.

Beyond that, this book is meant to take that inner Awakening into its continuing unfoldment so you can know by direct experience, beyond all belief and imagination, the ultimate reality of existence. This book is for all seekers and finders of Truth. If you have already awakened, this book will help deepen your experience and add a wider dimension to your knowledge and understanding.

This book is a true account of the field of Consciousness itself, beyond the mind, body and all perceptions, and beyond the false sense of a separate individual self. It is only necessary to read and reread these pages with a simple, innocent, open mind to gain the benefit. Your real Self is infinite, unbounded and beyond everything you now experience yourself to be. It is the most important part of your existence, and the doorway to the unfoldment of the ultimate reality of life. To awaken to that unseen unbounded, absolute reality of all existence, and to open to its total divine reality, is the ultimate purpose of your life.

≈≈≈

PART I

THE INNER BEING

CHAPTER ONE

REALITY

PATH TO REALITY

Who am I? Why am I here? How did I get here? What is the real purpose of my existence? What is the universe? What is my role in the overall scheme of things? What is the ultimate reality? What is God? What is enlightenment? What happens after enlightenment? What is life all about?

If you have been asking yourself questions like this, and have chosen to read this book, it means the time is right for you to know the truth about your life, and about the true reality of the world and universe. You may think the world you are experiencing through your mind and senses is real; you may think you play only a small part in the overall scheme of things. But you are about to discover what the world really is and just how important you really are.

Our personal life experience and perceptions of the world provide us with a seemingly convincing picture of reality. But what was once thought to be known for certain has been found to be untrue—the world is not flat and the sun does not revolve around the earth. Everything we believe, perceive and know now, is bound to change in the light of greater knowledge and awareness, especially when faced with a profound truth that resonates deep within the inner core of our being.

Discoveries in science continue to force us to question the validity of our concepts and beliefs, and even our perceptions of the reality we experience through our senses. The more science probes into the finer quantum fabric of life, the more it is realized that the world and universe is not at all what it appears to be. Quantum mechanics is the underlying basis of all physical life and a deeper reality of our own existence, and yet it is completely mystifying to the scientific mind. The quest to discover what Reality is through science is, in a sense, a spiritual quest.

Real spiritual pursuit is not based on faith or belief. Real spiritual pursuit is the search for the *direct experience* of the true reality of life. The spiritual path is a *Path to Reality*—a path to reality as it really is, not the way it appears. Anyone who is investigating into the hidden realities of life (from the subtleties of the quantum world, to the cosmic dimensions of outer space, to the inner expanse of the mind, heart and consciousness) is on a spiritual path. Anyone seeking Truth is on a spiritual path. Anyone seeking real peace, freedom and joy is on a spiritual path. We are all on a spiritual path whether we realize it or not.

But it is not possible to experience the true reality of life, or to achieve a lasting state of real peace and freedom, without first awakening to the true reality of your Self. Your real Self is the pure Awareness that enables experience to be experienced. It is the Awareness that impartially observes all experience. That impartial Observer is not your thinking mind or intellect, or anything you have been referring to as "me". It is that which observes the "me". Your real Self is the silent Observer of your thoughts, feelings, actions and perceptions. Without the direct experience of the true unbounded reality of your Self, it is not possible to know the true reality of the world or universe.

Your real Self is the innermost sense of being and existing, the sense that "I am, I exist". It is the most intimate, essential aspect of your life and the fundamental reality of your existence. Your real Self is closer to you than your body and senses, closer than your own mind and intellect, closer than your emotions and feelings, closer than your own breath. Ordinarily you do not experience it or even realize it is there. It is so subtle, so abstract, that its true reality is imperceptible to the mind. It has been overshadowed by thoughts, feelings, sensations, perceptions and experiences. The direct experience of your true Being has been obscured in the act of living due to the overshadowing influence of perceptions and experiences, and identification with your body and mind.

And yet, that pure sense of Being is who you really are. It is your real Self. It is the source of your existence. Without the sense of Being, the reality you are experiencing now would not exist. You would not exist. Without the sense of Being, nothing would exist for anyone. It is the one undeniable, irrevocable, irrefutable absolute truth. Without a sense of simply Being, there would be no one to perceive the experience of existence.

Your sense of Being, my sense of Being, everyone's sense of Being, is the same sense of Being. It is the one common experience of all beings who have ever, or will ever live. Everyone experiences the sense that they exist. When associated with the mind and body, this universal sense of Being appears to be a personal sense of being. In reality, it is the same one universal sense of Being and existing experienced by every living thing. It is the unbounded, eternal, pure sense of Being, the true absolute essence of all life.

This universal sense of Being is pure Awareness, pure Consciousness. It is the same conscious awareness you are experiencing now, only experienced on its own level by itself, not associated with or overshadowed by thoughts, emotions, sensations or perceptions. It is beyond your mind and body, and yet it pervades, permeates and animates your mind and body and your total life experience. It is the reason you are awake and aware. Responsible for all things known and seen, pure Awareness itself remains unknown and unseen.

Pure Awareness cannot be perceived by the senses, understood by the mind, or felt by the feelings; yet it is that by virtue of which your senses can perceive, your mind can think, and your feelings can feel. It is that which is enabling you to think, feel and perceive right now. It is neither objective nor subjective; it is the timeless silent source of all subjectivity and objectivity. It is unmanifest absolute universal pure Being. It exists on its own level, all by itself.

Pure Awareness is absolute Peace, boundless Freedom and innocent, pure Joy. Everyone experiences some degree of pure Awareness because it is the essential reality of Life. It is your real Self and the underlying basis, source and reason for your existence. Awakening to the direct abiding experience of *being* that absolute, unbounded, universal reality of all existence is called Self-Realization.

Self-Realization is the natural state of spontaneously maintaining unbounded pure Awareness within the boundaries of living. It is the essential first stage of awakening to full enlightenment and the true reality of what you, the world and universe really are, as described in detail in further chapters.

Self-Realization is not an intellectual realization, an attitude, a feeling or a belief. It is a deeply profound inner awakening that spontaneously occurs within the innermost core of your being as it awakens to its unbounded universal reality. It is not the result of faith, belief, understanding, study or practice. It happens beyond the mind, body, emotions and senses, and can only arise and awaken within you of its own accord. There is nothing you can do to make it happen. It happens naturally, when the time is right. It can happen to anyone at any time. It can happen to you.

If read with simple innocence and openness, without the intention to study or analyze, this book can act as a catalyst for that inner awakening, and for the continued unfoldment of consciousness.

AMNESIA

What if you woke up one morning and discovered that everything you believed, understood and experienced was not real? What if the world was not at all what it appeared to be? What if the person you thought you were, was not who you really are? What if you had been living your whole life as if in a dream? How would you feel? What would you do? Who would you be?

...

There once was a King who liked to disguise himself in the garb of a peasant so he could roam freely throughout his kingdom and see firsthand the concerns and needs of his people without being recognized. One day, while in disguise, he accidentally tripped and fell and was knocked unconscious. When he regained consciousness, he did not remember who or where he was. The blow to his head had caused amnesia.

He saw himself dressed in a peasant's clothes and believing himself to be one, he led the life of a peasant. In time, his pursuit for sustenance, livelihood, family, enjoyment and salvation consumed all his energy, and he lost the inclination to learn his true identity.

One night several years later, he dreamed that he was living in a grand palace made of gold and surrounded by everything he could ever desire. He knew it was just a dream, but the sights, sounds and fragrances felt so real and familiar, they rekindled in him the desire to find out who he really was.

When describing his dream to his friends, to his surprise and delight, he found out that such a palace existed, and he set out to find it. After warning him that the road to the palace was long and difficult, and that people of his status were not allowed in, his friends pointed him in the right direction.

The path to the palace was very hard and long indeed. He would have turned back in frustration many times, except that he noticed sights and sounds along the way felt familiar. After an arduous journey, he saw the palace in the distance. It was the palace of his dream. Elated, he increased his pace. As he approached, he saw an unguarded gate and entered.

As soon as he stepped his foot through the gate into the palace gardens, in a flash, he remembered who he really was. He was overwhelmed with peace, joy, happiness and bliss. He then realized that it was not the palace that was the dream, but it was his life of striving and suffering as a peasant that had been the dream. He had been the King all along.

...

If you have not yet awakened to being unbounded pure Awareness, whether or not you realize it, you are just like the King. You have become so entangled in your thoughts, feelings and perceptions that you have forgotten who you really are. You have become so involved in your search for happiness, freedom, betterment, status, wealth, family and salvation that you have forgotten the real purpose of your existence.

THE REAL WORLD

Our experience tells us that the world is made of concrete physical things, and this appears to be the undeniable reality. But we know from physics that this is not true. Everything in the world and universe, including our own bodies, is made of tiny atoms and subatomic particles that are not at all physical. They are infinitesimally small invisible whirling vortexes of energy that have no clearly defined physical boundaries, and could even extend to infinity, as far as anyone knows. The essential constituents out of which everything is composed have no real physical structure or boundaries. They are frequencies of energy, not tangible things.

Moreover, the more physicists delve into these subatomic particles, the more they realize there is really nothing there. There is a void, a quantum vacuum. This vacuum state is not empty, but alive with virtual particles constantly popping in and out of existence, somehow miraculously creating the appearance of physical matter. All the physical things we see around us, that seem to be so real, have no real material structure. Even though we perceive physical objects, there is nothing in the universe that can be said to have any real material physicality. Something made of non-physical material cannot truthfully be called real matter.

Our perception of the solid physical world around us, including our own bodies is, at best, only a partial experience of reality. The knowledge of quantum physics alone is enough to make any intelligent person realize that there is much more to life than meets the eye.

Not only is our experience of the world incomplete according to physics, according to neuroscience our perception of the world through our senses is also incomplete. We experience everything in the physical world through the five senses, and yet our senses provide us with only a small fraction of the information that is actually out there. Our eyes only detect visible light which is less than 1% of the known electromagnetic spectrum. Our ears hear less than 1% of the auditory spectrum. The rest of our senses are equally limited.

Not only are our senses limited, but our conscious mind is limited in its ability to use the information gathered by the brain and senses. It is well known that we use a very small portion of our brain's potential. It is estimated that our brains process billions of bits of information per second from our body and surroundings, but our conscious mind only uses a tiny portion of this information stream (approx. 2000 bits) to construct our experience of reality. With such limited capacity, how can we be certain we are experiencing the world, and even our own bodies, accurately?

What is even more surprising, our senses do not even directly perceive what appears to be out there. When you look at something (this page and the surrounding room, for example) it appears as though your eyes are seeing what is in front of you. But according to neuroscience, our eyes do not actually see the world around us. Our eyes are like sensors that pick up electromagnetic energy from the surrounding environment. That electromagnetic energy is converted into electrochemical signals by specific cells in the retina and then travel through the optic nerve to the visual cortex of the brain where they are interpreted into something meaningful to us. That information is flashed onto our conscious mind and only then do we experience what appears to be out there.

The forms and images of the world we perceive are actually created in our brain. They are our mind's interpretation of the electrochemical signals produced in our brains. Our eyes are not seeing the world; it is our brain that does the seeing.

This greatly differs from our experience. We think we are directly perceiving our surroundings through our senses. But we are only experiencing the images created by the electrical and electrochemical activity in our brains. Everything you see in your surroundings now is happening in the visual cortex of your brain. You only perceive your mind's interpretation of what exists. This is true for all your senses.

In other words, rather than directly experiencing a real objective world, you are actually experiencing the *subjective experience* of what appears to be a real objective world. This may come as a surprise to you, but you have never *directly* experienced anything. You only experience indirectly. You have only ever perceived your perceptions of the world, not the direct experience of the world itself.

Not only do your senses give you an incomplete picture of reality, they don't even directly perceive what is really out here. Not only is the world out here your mind's interpretation of the activity in your brain, your conscious mind only provides a tiny picture of reality due to the limited use of the brain's capacity.

There are other scientific findings and theories that question our perception of reality, but even with these basic facts, it cannot be said with absolute scientific certainty that the world exists in the way we experience it. Your obvious experience of the "real world" out here is very incomplete. Suffice it to say, nothing is as it appears to be.

But, at least, you know one thing for certain: you know who you are, you know you are real, you know you are the person experiencing the world around you... or do you?

THE REAL YOU

You are awake and aware. You are reading this book. You are aware of the objects around you, the room and the chair you're sitting on. You can look outside and see the world.

You are obviously the person who is experiencing the world around you. You are the observer, the experiencer, the subject; and this book, the room and everything else, are objects of experience. This is so obvious that we take its truth for granted.

But, let's look a little closer...

The person you think you are is who you are, of course, but is it your real Self? Remember, we are trying to find out who "You" really are. When you say "I am this person", we are trying to find out who that "I" is—who the subject, the experiencer is, who the real Self is. Is the Self your body, mind, intellect, memory, intuition, personality, emotions? All of this, or none of this? What is that pure inner sense of Being and existing? What is the Self? Where is it located? Who are you?

These are not easy questions to answer. The search for the true essence of our inner Being has been the perennial quest of all great thinkers, philosophers and sages throughout time, so don't expect to define or locate it right at this moment. It is the most abstract aspect of your existence, yet it is by far the most essential. Without the sense of Being, you would not exist. It may not be so easy to identify what your real inner Self actually is, but it is very easy to identify what it is not.

Your real Self is the subject, and everything else is an object of experience. But obviously, the subject cannot be an object of its own experience. You are not the book you are reading. You are not the chair you are sitting on. If you are aware of something, then it is an object of your awareness, not the subject, not your Self. Your real Self is the observer, the experiencer, the Awareness aware of the object.

So, let us take a closer look, and see if you really are the person you think you are. Let's start with your body.

Naturally, you are aware of your body...

You are aware of its sensations.

You feel the sensation of sitting on the chair.

You are aware of your breathing.

You are aware of your entire body.

So, if you can be aware of your body, then technically speaking, you are not your body. Your body is an object in your awareness, not the subject, not the Self. You are the *experiencer* of your body.

18

You may not have thought of it in this way before, but it is undeniably true. You are not your body.

You are the "Observer" of your body.

Your personality is the sum total of the person you experience yourself as being. Though ofttimes quite a complicated construct of traits, qualities and characteristics, it is still very easy to be aware of it. Your personality is clearly an object of your experience. It is not the subject. Technically, you are not your personality; you are the Observer of it.

The same is true of your feelings and emotions because, as you know, whenever any emotion arises, it's hard not to be aware of it. Emotions are also objects of your experience. They are not the subject, not who "You" are.

You may think it is your mind that is aware of all this. But if you are completely silent and still, you will notice that you can be aware of your mind thinking.

Take a few minutes, close your eyes, and quietly notice the thoughts in your mind...

When you are innocently awake and alert, you can be aware of your own mind thinking.

Your mind is thinking and reacting to these words right now as you are reading...

You may even notice your intellect analyzing this.

You are subtly aware of your conscious thinking mind.

Your thinking mind, irrespective of the content of your thoughts, is an object of your experience. It is not the observer, not the subject, not your Self.

You can even be aware of your attention shifting from the page, to the body, to your mind, to your emotions, to your entire personhood, to the surroundings.

Your entire body and mind are objects in awareness, they are not the subject, not your Self.

Upon close investigation, we discover that who "You" really are is not your body, your personality, your feelings, your emotions, your imagination, your thinking mind or intellect, your attention, or your entire personhood.

This simple exercise in logic shows that everything you have been referring to as "me" is in reality, an object of experience. It is not the subject, not the real Observer.

It is not who "You" really are.

The one foundational assumption that your life experience (and all science, religion and philosophy) is based upon is that the person is the subject, and the world out there is an object. This is found to be fundamentally incorrect.

The person you think you are is just as much an object of experience as your perceptions of the world.

If you can look from a place of silent clear awareness deep within, you will discover that this is undeniably true. The simple fact is: "You" are not the person you thought you were. You are the *Awareness* that is aware of the person.

You are Awareness itself.

So, what is that observing Awareness? Where is it? Who are You? You may want to ponder this for a while...

It does not matter how long you try to figure this out, you won't be able to find the observer of your mind by looking for it with your mind. The real Observer is beyond the range of the mind that is searching for it. The mind is not capable of knowing that which gives it its ability to know.

But, that Observer is obviously there. It is your innermost wakeful pure Awareness and your intimate sense of being. (Don't confuse the words "pure Awareness" with the mind. Mind awareness is the experience of the *content* in Awareness, not Awareness itself.) Even though the Observer is aware of your mind and body, it is not your mind, your body or anything you thought you were. What you have been referring to as "myself" has actually been an object of experience all along.

To sum up: your experience that the world and universe is the solid physical reality it appears to be, is not true; your experience that your senses are directly perceiving what is in front of you is not true; and the experience that you are the person experiencing the world out there, is also not true. You are the Observer of it all.

In the so-called "normal" waking state of consciousness, we do not experience the true reality of the world around us. We do not perceive the real mechanics of experiencing it through the brain and senses, nor do we experience the true reality of the experiencer—the real Self.

You have been falsely identified with your mind and body, living in a world that only appears to be out there separate from you. You have not been experiencing reality as it is. Like the King with amnesia, you have been living a life lost to the experience of who and what you really are.

To put it rather bluntly: *You have been living an illusion.*

THE ELUSIVE ENLIGHTENMENT

Even though you may not have realized it yet, you are seeking enlightenment. Enlightenment is the natural state of fully awakened Consciousness. It is not a mystical experience or an altered state of consciousness. It is not a belief, an attitude, mood, or imagination. It is the direct experience of being who You really are, not who you think you are. It is directly experiencing reality as it actually is, not the way it appears to be.

The silent Observer of your mind/body has been there all along, but it has been so overshadowed by your thoughts, feelings and perceptions that ordinarily you are not aware of it. This is because the mind functions within time and space whereas the Observer is timeless. Everyone experiences a deep inner sense of being that has not changed—a timeless inner sense of, "I am the same self I was as far back as I can remember, even though everything about me has changed many times over."

This non-changing inner sense of Being is your real self, only not yet clearly awakened to the unbounded timeless reality of its Self. It only seems vague and illusive because it has been almost completely overshadowed by the changing aspects of your mind, body and life experience. Yet it is the nearest, dearest, and most intimate essence of who you are.

It is pure Awareness, your innate sense of existing. It is so close to you that your eyes cannot see it, your mind cannot know it, and your emotions cannot feel it. Yet you know it's there, because it is who You really are. It is the deepest, innermost true sense that "I am", that "I exist", beyond the experience that "I am this person". It is the non-doing, non-moving impartial silent Observer of all your thoughts, sensations, feelings and perceptions. It is the clear wakeful pure Awareness in which all experiences happen, and it is that by virtue of which all experience can happen. It underlies and pervades your mind, body and all your perceptions.

It is underlying and pervading the space through which your eyes are seeing the words on this page right now...

You may recall a moment in your life, when, for no particular reason, you became so present in the moment that time seemed to stand still, and you felt a deep sense of peace, expanded awareness, boundless freedom and exquisite joy. Almost everyone has had a glimpse of this at some time in their life even if only for a split second. At that time, you were momentarily drawn out of your thinking mind and into a clearer experience of pure Awareness itself, your real Self.

That timeless sense of being fully awake and present in the moment is a glimpse of pure Awareness. It is your pure sense of Being. It is who you really are beyond the entanglement with the person you think you are. That non-changing, non-doing pure Awareness is always present in everyone, but it is not consciously experienced. This is because it is not an experience: it is the Observer of all experience. It is the pure field of Awareness in which all experience happens. It is your real Self, experienced on its own level all by itself, unaffected or tainted by the inner or outer changing modes of the body, mind, emotions and perceptions.

We have been so identified with the changing aspect of ourselves, and so out of touch with the innermost non-changing aspect of ourselves, that we may even doubt its existence. Yet it is by far the most important part of who we are, for without that non-changing sense of being and existing, the mind, body and everything we think is real, would not exist.

All your life, through your every endeavor, you have been seeking happiness, peace, freedom and fulfilment—very likely, without much lasting success. In case it has not dawned on you by now, you will not find what you are looking for out there in the world. It does not exist there. The world is always changing and is not at all what it appears to be.

You will not find happiness by looking inward to your body, mind, or emotions either. They too are always changing and not the true reality of your Self. You have been trying to find something permanent by searching in the changing, impermanent field of life where it simply does not exist.

The ever-changing life experience is so dominant and obvious that we seldom question its validity. But there is a great discrepancy between our experience of reality and what reality actually is. The world appears to be flat, but in reality, it is round. The sun appears to go around the earth, but in reality, the earth goes around the sun. The world appears to be made of solid matter, but in reality, it is made of atoms that are nonphysical whirling points of empty space.

It appears as though you are directly perceiving the world through your senses, but in reality, your perception is your mind's interpretation of the electrical signals in your brain. The world is not out there separate from you as it appears. It is actually in your own mind, your own consciousness. Your senses appear to be in your body, but in reality, the experience of your body is possible only due to your senses. Your mind may appear to be in your body, but in reality, your body is in your mind. There is a much deeper reality of our own mind and consciousness to which we may not yet be awake.

We think we have a physical body with a temporary existence. But in reality, according to physics, our bodies are made of atoms formed within the first minutes after the Big Bang over 13.7 billion years ago. The causal quantum dynamics that formed the universe is contained within your body right now. The true reality of your body is not that it is a physical, individual, ephemeral body, but that it is ancient, cosmic and universal. There is a universal quantum field reality of our body and brain to which we have not been awake.

You have been experiencing that "I am my mind and body", but in reality, you are the Observer of your mind and body. The Observer of your mind, your real Self, is pure Awareness.

Awareness is not in your mind; your mind is in Awareness. Your real Self is not in your body/mind, as it appears. Your body/mind is in your Self. There is a universal, boundless dimension to our self to which we have not been awake.

Our so-called "normal" experience of reality is something we have all blindly accepted as true, but it is far from reality. Nothing is the way it appears. Is it any wonder that so few people in the world live in a lasting state of real inner peace, happiness and fulfilment? Is it any wonder that the world is in the state it is?

No matter what you do, or how much you learn and achieve in life, it will only bring temporary joy and fulfilment. Inevitably, you will be left with the sense that something is missing. Thanks to science and our own intelligent introspection, we can now comprehend that there is much more to life than we have been experiencing. And, it is now within our grasp.

What we have been missing is the direct abiding experience of the non-changing reality of our innermost Being. Pure peace, freedom and joy has been hidden deep within our experience all along, overshadowed by the ever-changing mind, emotions and perceptions. That pure peace and freedom is our real Self.

Some people may argue that the only way to find real peace and happiness is through God. Who can argue with that? But if you do not know who You really are, how can you possibly expect to know what God, or anything else, really is? Only by awakening, to the absolute non-changing reality of your innermost Being, can the true reality of anything be known. Though hidden from view, the absolute reality of your true Self is not only open to direct experience, but can be permanently lived in daily life.

Awakening to your real Self happens within the innermost core of your being. An unmistakable spontaneous shift takes place, from predominantly experiencing the changing aspect of yourself, to predominantly experiencing the non-changing aspect of your Self. It is a shift from being the person you think you are (bound by thoughts, emotions and experiences) to being the unbounded silent, pure Awareness in which all experience is happening. It is a permanent shift to being the unbounded peace, freedom and joy of your real Self, no longer overshadowed by life experiences, however pleasant or unpleasant. It is waking up to who you really are.

Everything you have ever experienced in life, whether physical, mental, emotional, or spiritual, has only been experienced within, and because of, Consciousness. Conscious Awareness is the vehicle of all experience. When you directly experience the true reality of your Self as unbounded pure Awareness itself, you live from that perspective. The doorway opens to a completely new dimension of life lived in peace, freedom and completeness, advancing quickly in the direction of full Enlightenment and the finer perception of the deeper divine reality of life as it really is.

≈≈≈

CHAPTER TWO

LISTENING

INNOCENT LISTENING

Pure Awareness is beyond the mind, body, senses and feelings, and cannot be known by study, practice, understanding, faith or belief. It cannot be described or understood in words. It is the underlying source of the mind that is trying to understand it, and that by virtue of which the mind can function. Words describing pure Awareness, when understood by the mind, can only create concepts. Concepts are just concepts, not reality.

The mind's concepts about enlightenment are either incomplete or incorrect. The mind, which is limited to time and space, seems to think that it can awaken to timeless pure Awareness by knowing or doing something within time and space. It has the tendency to create unrealistic expectations. There is no greater barrier to enlightenment than a mind that thinks it knows what enlightenment is.

If you are a long-term seeker who has not yet Awakened, then perhaps it is your concepts about enlightenment that are holding you back. You should know that *it is not the person that becomes enlightened.*

It is the Observer of the person, your real innermost self, that awakens to its true unbounded reality.

That is why it is called Self-Realization. It is not an intellectual realization, a feeling, or a perception. The inner self awakens to its boundless Self. It is an unmistakable spontaneous awakening to the unbounded reality of your real true Self that occurs within the innermost core of your Being.

The "inner self" is not the "higher self". The "higher self" is the finer qualities of your personality and finer feelings, whereas, the "inner self" is the pure wakeful Awareness in which the higher self and lower self both exist—in which everything exists.

If you are seriously interested in Awakening, before continuing, you will have to learn how to read this book in such a way that you can get around the tendencies of your own mind. Words coming from the level of pure Awareness, if heard or read with simple innocence and openness, can help to catalyze the Awakening to the true unbounded reality of your Self.

The real Self is the silent, pure Awareness that is simply awake and aware, beyond your thoughts, feelings and perceptions. From the perspective of the mind, pure Awareness is so vague and abstract that it is easily missed, or not experienced at all. It needs to be brought more concretely into the foreground of experience. This cannot be done by the mind, intellect, emotions or senses, which are all objects of experience, not the subject. Only the Self, the real subject, can know itself. It can only arise of its own accord when the time is right.

In order for the true reality of your Self to arise, it is necessary to be very simple, innocent and open. If your mind is too full of knowledge, concepts, judgments, beliefs or imaginations, there is no room left for Truth. The unbounded reality of your true innermost Being cannot emerge when concepts and ideas are in the way.

There are so many versions of "Truth" available these days that it is natural to be wary. However, it is not possible to be completely innocent and open when the mind is continually on guard. For real Truth to be known, at some point, real trust must arise.

This book has nothing to do with belief, imagination, religion or philosophy. It deals only with reality as it is. Your innermost pure sense of Being is the basis of that reality. This book is about your innermost Being, your true Self, which is the most intimate and beautiful part of you. Becoming acquainted with it is completely safe, so there is nothing to fear. As you read on, some of these words are bound to penetrate beyond your mind to the innermost core of your being, and a deeper inner knowing will spontaneously arise. Relax and allow this to happen.

When you read this book, listen to the words from a place of silence deep within, not from the mind. There is a place of pure wakeful, alert Awareness within you that just sees. It sees your own mind, emotions and entire personhood.

It just silently watches...

It is watching your thoughts and feelings right now

It sees your body — your breath — your slightest sensations

It sees your innermost doubts and fears

It is the silent Seer within.

It is an impartial, non-judgmental, protective place of inner silence and peace. It is the non-changing, non-moving, non-doing wakefulness of the sense of pure Being. True awakening happens beyond all thoughts, feelings, sensations and perceptions, deep within the realm of that innermost silent sense of simply Being.

This book speaks to that pure sense of Being, the silent Seer in you, not to your mind or emotions. To get the most out of it, innocently read and listen from that silent space of non-judgmental clear Awareness within you and be innocently awake to what your mind is doing while you read. It's not necessary to try to control your mind. If it agrees with what is said, let it agree. If it disagrees, let it disagree. If it is questioning, let it question. If it is judging, let it judge. If it becomes defensive, let it become defensive.

Let the mind do whatever it wants to do while staying innocently awake to what it is doing from that silent place of inner peace within you. At times you may be completely caught up in the mind's gymnastics. At other times, you will see clearly that you are its Observer.

Shifting from being identified with the mind, to being the silent Witness of the mind, is a profound yet subtle thing. It is not something your mind can do. Only the Observer of the mind, your real Self, can experience itself. However, the shift to being the real Observer does not arise from the process of self-observation. There is a big difference between observing the mind with the intellect versus *being* the pure Awareness that is naturally awake to the mind. When the intellect tries to observe the mind, there is effort involved and this can divide the mind, making it less effective. This is not the real Observer. It is your mind trying to observe itself.

The real Observer is naturally and effortlessly observing at all times from a place of pure clarity and simplicity. If you remain simple, innocent and open, the real Observer will arise of its own accord. You will know you are listening from that inner silent space when you can see your own mind thinking.

When you are awake to the voice in your head analyzing, agreeing, disagreeing and forming opinions, but not caught up in it or judging it, you are listening from that inner silent space.

When awareness is innocently awake and alert, and thoughts, emotions and perceptions effortlessly flow through you, you are listening from that silent space.

When some profound truth resonates deep within, you are listening from that inner silent space.

When you are dominantly experiencing an inner calm and peace, and the silent Presence around you is so palpable that it cannot be denied, you are listening from that silent space of pure Being.

The words in this book are directed to that silent witnessing Awareness, not your mind or intellect. Innocently being awake to what your mind is doing, and allowing it to do whatever it is doing, creates an opening for your innermost self to hear itself speaking through these words.

This is what is meant by "innocent listening". Only your innermost being can innocently, effortlessly be awake to the mind. That innermost being is the simple non-moving, alert awareness through which your thoughts, feelings and perceptions are moving right now. It is that silent, non-doing pure Awareness that awakens to its unbounded infinite reality. Your mind and intellect have no part in the process.

Being aware that you are the observer of your mind is a first step in the direction of the true Awakening. In order for the real Awakening to occur, another more profound shift takes place. This shift happens when the Observer observes itself.

The inner self (the witness to the mind) recognizes its Self on its own level, all by itself, beyond all thoughts, feelings, and perceptions. When it does, a natural split occurs between the mind/body and the Observer of the mind/body, between the contents of awareness and Awareness itself. If the time is right for you, a subtle question may arise: "Who am I? Am I this person, or am I that vast Presence that seems to be overtaking me?" At this point, an unmistakable shift can take place in the sense of who you are. The individual self-sense disappears and awakens to being the unbounded field of pure Awareness itself in which all perception and experience happens. You have come back home to your natural state of being pure peace and the boundless freedom and joy of simply Being. It is what you have always been, but have not been awake to.

This can only arise naturally, of its own accord. Until it does, just be simple, innocent and open. Continue to read this book from that place of inner silence deep within. Innocently notice what your mind is doing and be awake to the Stillness and Presence in the room around you.

PRESENT MOMENT PURE AWARENESS

The present moment is very elusive to the mind. The mind is so busy with its stream of thoughts, all vying for attention and in such a rush to get to the next moment, that the simple timeless, present-moment pure Awareness, in which all of that is happening, remains unseen.

Yet, there is *only* the present moment. Everything that has ever happened in the past, present and future, has always happened in the present moment of Now. But, because the thinking mind, emotions, perceptions and experiences dominate the attention, the present moment pure Awareness, in which it is all happening, has remained overshadowed, elusive, and rarely, if ever, directly experienced.

Real present moment pure Awareness is not the concept of "being present in the moment" that is so popular these days. It does not mean focusing on what is happening right now in this moment of space and time. Present moment Awareness is beyond space and time. It is timelessness itself. It is the silent non-doing timeless pure Awareness in which everything is happening. Present moment pure Awareness means that the silent seer within, your real Self, is awake to itself.

It is that silent impartial witnessing Awareness that is awake right here now, silently watching your eyes as they move across this page reading these words...

Watching the thoughts in your mind

Watching your intellect analyze these words

Watching your emotions and sensations

Silently watching your mind and body...

The real "present moment" is that non-moving, non-doing, timeless *pure Awareness* through which the past, present and future move.

If you can be simple and innocent, as you continue reading, you will notice the silence within you and the Stillness in the surrounding space begin to deepen. Stillness and silence are the effect produced by the nearness to pure Awareness, which is the simple silent boundless sense of pure Being. Your true Self, beyond all thoughts and experience, is that non-moving, non-doing silent still Awareness. All thoughts, feelings, perceptions and experiences happen within the timeless Stillness of the silent, wakeful pure Awareness of your innermost Being.

The experience of the silent peace and freedom of your true Being is completely natural. Everyone experiences some value of it in the simple act of living. Every innocent experience of peace, freedom and joy is ultimately a small taste of the timelessness of your innermost Being.

Having been so overshadowed by the phenomena of life experience, we attribute any glimpse into the real peace and joy of pure Being to the life circumstance that appeared to have brought it about. That life circumstance simply triggered an experience of the pure peace and freedom of your real Self. Life is full of these triggers. They are gifts from nature.

Remember the sense of calm and peace you felt lying on a quiet beach in the sun, its soothing rays warming your skin, a gentle breeze caressing your body, the waves lapping the shore drawing you deep into the inner silence of your being?

Remember that stroll through the quiet forest, enjoying nature, sensing the profound silence and stillness all around you?

Remember those calm, peaceful, soothing feelings nourishing your soul?

Just the memory of any serene experience instantly brings back some degree of the experience that was felt at the time.

The reason memories trigger this feeling is because that inner peace has never left you. It has always been there. It is here right now. It is within you. It is all around you. It was not in the forest or on the beach. It is the very nature of the timeless, present-moment pure Awareness of your inner Self, beyond the activity of your mind, emotions and perceptions.

Your innermost pure sense of Being *is* pure peace, joy and freedom. The peace you attributed to the experience you were having was within you all along, only it was overshadowed by the mind, objects of perception and drama of life. That experience you had served as a catalyst to expose the peace of your innermost Being to your awareness.

Your true Self *is* the timeless, present-moment pure Awareness in which all time and space is moving. It is that, by virtue of which, all experience happens. Timeless, present-moment pure Awareness is what you have been throughout your entire life only you have not been awake to it. That deep inner sense of pure Being has never changed. The sense that "I am the same self I have been since childhood, even though everything else about me has changed" is a vague experience of that time-less, present-moment pure Awareness.

When the real Awakening happens, that non-changing ab-solute aspect of yourself is no longer a vague, abstract experi-ence. The peace, freedom and joy of pure Being becomes the unshakable dominant reality of your existence, regardless of what happens in your body, mind or life experience. All life happens within that non-changing boundless reality of your Being.

After awakening, you remain the same person you have al-ways been, only the changing aspect of yourself moves into the background of experience, and the non-changing reality of your true Self moves into the foreground of experience, where it is meant to be. You simply come back to your natural state of being.

Awakening to the unbounded reality of being pure Aware-ness is not a mystical, esoteric experience or an altered state of mind. It is the most natural state of Being. If you have ever been up high in the mountains overlooking an expanse of dis-tant mountain peaks on the horizon, what can become more dominant than the spectacular scene itself is a sense of over-whelming vastness, expansion and freedom. Your awareness expands outside the ordinary limits of your mind/body. And perhaps, if you are lucky, you may get a glimpse into the maj-esty of your true Being.

That experience quickly fades, however, and you soon shrink back into your mind and body. But, that fleeting sense of expanded awareness, of being boundless and free, is your natural state of being, and it is the only thing that is truly real... as you will soon discover.

The clarity of the boundless, timeless reality of your true inner Being has been lost in the experience of living. It only needs to be gently coaxed out of obscurity and brought back into the forefront of life experience. This book is written for that very purpose. It is not meant for gaining knowledge or information. It is designed to take you gradually, step by step, into deeper degrees of the silent, wakeful Awareness of your inner Being and to draw it into the foreground of experience, so that the possibility can arise for you to at least get a clearer glimpse of the unbounded reality of your true Self.

All you need to do is to innocently follow the simple directions given throughout this book and allow the experience to deepen. When the boundless reality of your innermost Being begins to arise, its Stillness and Presence will be so palpably felt in the room around you that nothing else will matter. As you continue to read, just be simple, innocent and open, and it will happen all by itself.

Sit comfortably, relax, and allow whatever is, to be, just as it is. Let go of your ideas and concepts about enlightenment for the time being...

Let go of the memory of past blissful experiences

Let go of what has been happening in your life

Let go of whatever you have to do in the future

Let go of anticipation

Let go of desire

Let go of seeking

Let go of everything, just for now, and allow yourself to enter into the silent space beyond it all—into the timeless, present-moment pure Awareness of the unbounded, eternal reality of your true Being.

INTO THE SELF

Read this slowly, and simply be with whatever arises.
Innocently notice the Stillness in the room...

There is a Stillness, a silent Presence all around you

It is a beautiful, peaceful Stillness

It is everywhere — within you — surrounding you

A boundless ocean of silent peace...

Initially it may be subtle, but the more you innocently let go
and allow, the more palpable it becomes.

Relax and allow everything to be just as it is, without trying
to do anything or change anything.

No need to look for anything or try to make a mood out of
this.

Let go of all your preconceived notions and concepts for the
time being and remain simple, innocent and open.

Just let go of everything...

Don't resist anything
Don't encourage anything

Don't expect anything

Don't mind your thoughts, sensations or emotions

Sit back and relax

Allow everything to be just as it is...

As you continue to be easy and simple, your thoughts and feelings may begin to become less dominant, or they may temporarily become more dominant, and that's okay too.

They will soon subside.

You may notice some bodily sensations. If they are present, don't mind them, just adjust your position and innocently allow your attention to be with the sensations for a while. Then let go.

Soon they won't dominate your awareness as much, and you can begin to settle into a more quiet, peaceful state.

If you feel tired, close your eyes for a minute before continuing...

Now innocently notice the Silence and Stillness around you...

Be with that Stillness

Allow it to become more dominant

Relax

Take a deep breath

Just let go

Be with the Stillness in the space around you

All the things that were so important in your life don't seem to matter quite as much anymore. It's all beginning to move more into the background of experience.

The innocent simplicity of just being present in the moment is arising...

Be with that simple innocence

Be with the Stillness

Now, while your mind is reading these words, innocently be awake to everything in your peripheral vision...

Take in the full panorama of awareness all around you

Allow your attention be with the full range of vision

Effortlessly be awake to everything all at once

Innocently be awake to that wide range of awareness

Be with that expansion

Notice the increased Stillness...

Notice the heightened awareness...

There's more spaciousness

More alertness

The eyes open wider

There's more lightness

The mind is quieter

Awareness is more expanded

More alert

Be with that increased alertness

Now, notice your eyes moving across the page reading these words...

Reading is happening with less effort

Attention is effortlessly focused on the words

Thoughts no longer absorb your full attention

Be with that effortless centered attention

Now, notice the Stillness in the space between your eyes and the page...

It is all around you

It's everywhere

The surrounding space is Silent, Still and Spacious...

yet more subtly alive

There is a calm, peaceful ease...

yet a quiet excitement felt through the whole being...

a tangible alive Presence surrounds you

the boundaries of your awareness are expanded

it feels good

a smile spreads across your face

Be with that...

The expanded awareness you are beginning to experience is the same sense of expansion you experienced on the mountain top, gazing spellbound at the vast panorama. This experience of expanded awareness is a taste of the infinite freedom, joy, and vastness of the true reality of your real unbounded Self. It is a glimpse into the spaciousness of your inner Being, but it is also a glimpse into the ultimate reality of existence itself.

Everything, within you and all around you, is pervaded by this vastness of empty space. Space is everywhere. All visible matter is made of atoms and subatomic particles that are more than 99.99% empty space. Every cell, tissue and organ in your body, and everything in the world around you, is made of these whirling vortices of empty space.

That empty space is the same felt sense of expansion, spaciousness and aliveness you are experiencing right now.

That spacious alive Presence is infinitely vast and deep. Less than 4% of the universe is visible matter, and the remainder is composed of an unknown Dark Matter and Dark Energy, both of which are still a mystery to scientists. That unknown 96% of all matter and energy is not way out there in the universe somewhere separate from you. It is permeating your mind, body and all perceptions, and is found deep within your own consciousness in the silent depths of your Being. It is the hidden reality of your existence, the hidden reality of all existence.

If it were possible to visit all the billions of galaxies in the universe and gather all the sensory information there, it would still only amount to less than 4% of the known reality. Yet, if you could go deeply into the silent Presence and Stillness that is within and around you right now, it would be possible to experience the remaining hidden 96% of reality.

It may be impossible to travel the vast universe and gather all that information, but it is entirely possible to experience 100% of the true essence of all existence in the timeless reality of your own Being. The silent expanse of your own inner Being *is* unbounded pure Awareness itself. It is only due to this conscious Awareness itself that anything can be known, or even exist.

How is it that the physical body, the personal life-situation and the world have become such a dominant experience, when it is, in fact, such a small part of the reality of life? How is it that we have lost touch with the vast expanse of the true reality of our existence?

How did you lose the silent peace and freedom of the unbounded reality of your own Self?

CONDITIONING

You got trapped in your mind: trapped by thoughts, beliefs, memories, imaginations, emotions, sensations, perceptions and experiences. You missed the simple present-moment pure Awareness of your real Being in which all of that is happening. Like the king who had amnesia, you have forgotten who you really are. You have become so identified with your mind/body and life experience that the silent expansive vastness of your real Being is only a vague notion. It will continue to be only a vague notion until the true Awakening happens.

When the real Awakening happens, you directly experience *being* pure Awareness itself, the underlying source of all experience. The vastness of your real Self is no longer just a vague sense; it is the dominant reality of your life. That unbounded silent peace, freedom, and joy of pure Being is the ultimate basis of all existence.

The direct experience of *being* unbounded pure Awareness itself has been lost in the act of living due to conditioning. The habit of experiencing ourselves as separate individual people has become so deeply ingrained, that even if the inner witness observes the mind, it is still bound to the false idea of separateness.

It is not enough to be aware of the witness of the mind to break free from the mind's conditioned sense of individual "me" and "mine". The witness needs to experience its clear unbounded reality, beyond the mind, intellect, feelings and perceptions, in order to break free completely from its false identification.

As the space in a container (which is the same space outside the container) becomes freed when the container breaks, the witness sees itself on its own level all by itself and is freed from its false identification with the mind/body. It naturally awakens to being the unbounded, infinite pure Awareness it has always been. But the container, in your case, is just the idea that you are localized to an individual mind/body, not an ordinary idea, but a deep-seated, deeply ingrained idea due to years and years of conditioning.

That "I am my mind and body" has become such a deeply entrenched idea, that to suggest otherwise would sound insane to most people, especially since strengthening our sense of a separate individual self and its uniqueness is so lauded in our society. Most people are so strongly identified with their mind/body that they have absolutely no idea there is something observing it, much less that the Observer is unbounded and free, and is *who they really are.*

After years, decades, and perhaps lifetimes, of referring to the mind/body as "me", the real unbounded Self becomes increasingly constricted and identified with the mind and body. The natural sense of inner freedom, peace, and the joy of simply being, has become obscured. In early childhood, the innocent joy and freedom was more dominant than the individual personal ego sense. It was more as though you experienced yourself as simply *having* a body rather than *being* the body. Your experience at that time was much closer to reality.

We have been conditioned to experience ourselves as being the body rather than just having a body. We have taken personal ownership of everything that has happened to us throughout life. This has created deep emotional and psychological impressions in the mind, and imbalance in the body, causing the sense of Being to shrink into individuality and become completely identified with the body. This is especially true regarding life experiences that have caused deep pain and injury to the emotions and psychology.

See how easy it is to be drawn into the mind and out of the natural experience of expanded awareness, even now while reading this book. Think of all the years of conditioning and constant referral back to the "me" as being special or plain, good or bad, sensitive or tough, a winner or loser, etc. This constant labelling and indoctrination takes a toll. It has constricted us into such a strong sense of individual self that the peace, freedom and joy of our real unbounded Self has been reduced to only an occasional fleeting experience, or even completely lost altogether.

This is what happens when we have not been educated about the true reality of our Self. Society, in general, has no clear understanding of what enlightenment actually is, and is not qualified to teach us about it or open our minds to it. Quite the opposite, society has taught us to reinforce our sense of a separate individual "me". It has even tried to convince us that experiences of expanded awareness, boundless freedom, oneness and bliss are possibly psychological imbalances, or at best, mystical experiences or altered states of consciousness. Is it any wonder that enlightenment is clouded by imagination, mysticism and incomplete understanding?

The unfortunate consequence of this lack of knowledge and experience is a life lived in ignorance of its true unbounded divine reality. Living in the restricted sense of being just an individual person has become the complete extent of our existence. Yet, anyone willing to do a little intelligent introspection will soon realize the truth that: "I am the observer of my thoughts, not my thoughts". If you have an inner knowing, the direct experience, or even a sense that you are the observer of your mind/body, and that the Observer is unlocalized, you have already taken a step in the right direction. Let's take another step in the right direction right now.

Sit back, relax and again notice the Stillness all around you...

Innocently be with that Stillness

Being with the Stillness settles the mind

When the mind settles, the body relaxes

Be with the Stillness

Allow the mind and body to relax

Notice the deepening sensation of relaxation...

As the mind relaxes — the body relaxes
As the body relaxes — the mind relaxes

As the mind and body relax,
Stillness and Presence become more palpable.

Notice that Still Presence...

As the Presence becomes more palpable,

awareness becomes clearer, sharper,

attention becomes more effortlessly concentrated,

wakeful alertness increases

Now, from that place of quiet wakeful alertness, notice your mind thinking while reading this...

Your mind is repeating these words

Listen to your mind repeating these words

Your eyes are seeing these words

Your mind is repeating these words

Your intellect is analyzing

Your eyes are seeing

Your mind is thinking

Your intellect is analyzing

Eyes are seeing

Mind is thinking

Intellect is analyzing

Everything that is occurring in your mind is being seen from a place of silent, wakeful alertness...

Every sensation in your body is felt from that place of silent, wakeful alertness...

Every perception of the surroundings is perceived from that place of silent, wakeful alertness...

When experienced on its own level, free from the mind, that wakeful pure alertness is the uninvolved impartial Observer of all your thoughts, feelings, sensations and perceptions.

It is this silent impartial Observer of your mind and body that awakens to its unbounded universal reality when the real Awakening occurs.

The true unbounded reality of your innermost sense of Being has been entangled with your thoughts, feelings and perceptions, identified with your mind and body due to conditioning. Its true reality, which is infinite unbounded pure Awareness, has been lost to experience.

After clearly awakening to the unbounded reality of your real Self, you remain the same person as you were before, only the boundless freedom, peace and joy of your real Being, becomes the dominant reality of life. Your life experience is pervaded by an unshakable constant sense of peace, completeness, freedom and inner stability, irrespective of anything that occurs, whether negative or positive.

When real peace, freedom and joy are not the dominant reality of your existence, you are not experiencing your real Self. If you are not experiencing your real Self, how can you expect to live life in the manner it was designed to be lived? And, how can you possibly expect to comprehend and experience the true reality of the world and universe around you?

You are so much more than your thoughts, emotions, feelings, sensations and perceptions. You are the timeless, eternal present moment pure Awareness in which all that exists. You have been fooled by an appearance, an illusion, that has become your reality. You may appear to be just an individual person, but, in reality, you have always been unbounded pure Consciousness itself, the same one Self of everyone, and the underlying field of pure Awareness in which all perception and experience happens. Just like the king with amnesia, you have forgotten who you really are.

≈≈≈

CHAPTER THREE

CONSCIOUSNESS

THE NEW PARADIGM

You may have noticed that there are tremendous changes taking place in the world today. Changes seem to be happening at a faster pace than at any other time in our life, or perhaps even in recorded history. The world is in the process of going through a major paradigm shift. When it was discovered that the world was not flat, or that the sun did not go around the earth, that realization caused a major paradigm shift in the consciousness of society at the time. The general understanding of the world and solar system that was held, turned out to be false. But nothing changed. The world had always been round and had always been revolving around the sun. The change that took place happened only in the collective understanding and awareness.

That new perspective brought major upheavals to education, science, religion and the general world view of the time, not unlike the changes happening in the world today. We are now going through another major paradigm shift, but this shift is not taking place just in our conscious understanding and perception of the world. This shift is much more fundamental, radical and profound. It is happening beyond the mind in the innermost realm of Consciousness itself; it is a shift in the very foundation of our sense of reality itself.

This shift is a shift in the sense of who and what we really are. It's a shift from experiencing life from the perspective of the individual conditioned mind, to experiencing life from the perspective of unconditioned, unbounded Awareness. Though there have been people who have Awakened in every age, this shift is completely unprecedented and extremely profound in that it is happening on such a large scale at this time.

For the first time in recorded history, tens of thousands of people around the world are spontaneously awakening to the direct experience of being unbounded pure Awareness, rather than the individual self-serving ego. After clearly awakening to being Awareness itself, the wavering mind is no longer the controller. An unshakable inner stability and expanded clarity of awareness and comprehension take over. You are no longer caught in the small boundaries of ego, emotion and narrow thinking, which formerly clouded the vision and were the underlying cause of the majority of the problems in the world.

This is a dramatic change, and it is already starting to create a profound effect in the entire collective consciousness of the world. There is only one field of Consciousness. When one person awakens to being unbounded pure Awareness, it creates a ripple in the entire ocean of Consciousness, and the consciousness of everyone everywhere is instantaneously influenced and heightened. Consciousness is rising everywhere.

As the collective consciousness rises, the more fixed, contracted, earthbound qualities of personality initially resist this change. This accounts for the polarization we see in the world today. But this conflict and division is temporary and only appears problematic on the surface. On a deeper level, awareness is rising. People are beginning to see from a broader perspective and are less likely to hold on to old ideas, concepts, and beliefs that are not holistic, positive and progressive. A greater sense of cohesion, unity and harmony will be the natural result.

MIND, AWARENESS & CONSCIOUSNESS

Everything that has ever happened, or will ever happen, happens in consciousness. All thoughts, feelings, sensations and perceptions happen within consciousness. All discoveries, inventions, realizations, philosophies and beliefs have arisen from someone's consciousness. Nothing has ever been known, or could possibly be known, by anyone at any time, outside of consciousness. Without consciousness, nothing would exist for anyone anywhere. Consciousness is the prerequisite for the experience of life. It is the pure essence of life and the ultimate underlying basis of all existence.

The word "consciousness" is generally used in reference to the activity of the mind being conscious of, and synthesizing information about, the external world. Conscious awareness, attention, thinking, sensing, feeling, intuition, discrimination, memory, perception, are all activities of the mind. Everything we know and experience in time and space, is due to the activity of the conscious mind. But this is what the conscious mind *does*, not what Consciousness itself actually *is*.

What "Consciousness" itself actually is has eluded the grasp of great thinkers throughout the ages, and it remains the greatest mystery in science today. It's a mystery because, in the ordinary waking state, we are only aware of the objects and phenomena within our conscious awareness. We do not experience pure Consciousness itself, which is the *source and essence* of that awareness. The conscious mind functions within the limitations of time and space, whereas, Consciousness itself is the timeless source of time and space *and* the mind.

On its own level, beyond the mind, Consciousness is an unbounded infinite field of pure Awareness. It is the timeless eternal present moment of Now through which all time and space flow. It is the absolute non-moving, non-changing universal sense of pure Being. Everything that has ever happened or will ever happen, happens within it. It is that by virtue of which anything can happen.

Due to conditioning, the pure sense of Being has become constricted and limited to the individual mind/body, and its unbounded universal reality has been lost to direct experience. We have been so caught in our mind, body and changing life experience, that we do not experience the non-changing, timeless, universal reality of our real Being. Most people have no idea that it even exists. Everyone has conscious awareness, but in ordinary waking state consciousness, timeless pure Awareness itself and its mechanism of being conscious and aware, remain unknown.

Consciousness and Awareness are essentially the same, only pure Consciousness includes the *process* of being aware. Pure Consciousness is Awareness aware of itself. "Conscious awareness" is the activity of the mind perceiving and experiencing the body and world around you right now. "Pure Awareness" is the unseen unbounded silent field of pure Being in which all perceiving, thinking, feeling and experiencing are happening. "Pure Consciousness" is non-moving pure Awareness *and* its subtle internal activity of being conscious of itself (which creates and appears as all experience - Part III).

The source of the Stillness within and around you right now is the non-moving, non-doing field of your own unbounded pure Awareness; and the awareness of it is the conscious activity of your mind. Waking state consciousness is pure Consciousness identified with the individual mind, body and the objects and phenomena of perception.

If you are a little confused, don't pay much attention to the definition of these words. Consciousness can't be adequately described in words anyway. Just continue reading innocently and take it as it comes.

UNIVERSAL CONSCIOUSNESS

In the initial Awakening, Consciousness itself, your real Self, is released from its entanglement with the mind/body and is experienced on its own level as being infinitely unbounded and free. The innermost sense of Being awakens to being unbounded pure Awareness, the cause of the Stillness and Presence you sense around you right now. Awareness itself is no longer isolated to your mind/body. It is the unbounded screen upon which all thoughts, feelings and perceptions of the world are displayed. Your mind, body and all its perceptions have been within unbounded pure Awareness all along.

We all have different bodies, minds and personalities, but pure Awareness itself is the same for everyone. It is the pure sense of Being and existing and the same one universal Self of all. It is infinite, unbounded and eternal. When identified with the personal mind/body, the mind assumes that the inner sense of Being is individual. But, the thinking mind is actually an object of experience, and it cannot possibly know whether the innermost Being is individual or universal. It can only have a belief or concept about it, but it cannot know for certain until the real Awakening happens.

True Awakening and Enlightenment have been lost to mainstream society and replaced by a multitude of concepts, beliefs, imaginations and misunderstandings. But, concepts and beliefs, no matter how dear, are just the concepts and beliefs of the mind. They are not reality. You are not the mind. You are the Observer of the mind. Only when the innermost sense of being clearly observes its Self, without interference from the mind, can it awaken to its unbounded universal reality. Only the *real Self* can know itself.

Set aside your concepts and beliefs for the time being. It's not necessary to make something mystical out of the most intimate part of you. Universal Consciousness is the simple, natural, most intimate reality of your inner being. When freed from the false identification with the mind, your inner being is found to be infinite, unbounded, universal Consciousness.

Space is space, air is air, no matter at what point it is being experienced. Consciousness is Consciousness, Awareness is Awareness, the sense of Being is the sense of Being, regardless of who is experiencing it or what is being experienced. There is only one universal sense of Being. It is the universal one Self of all. Your innermost sense of being *is* universal Being.

Being universal Consciousness does not mean you lose your sense of individuality. Universality *includes* individuality. The boundless universal reality of your Being has been underlying and pervading your individual life all along. It is only because your sense of self has been identified with the mind, body and all of your perceptions that its universal reality appears to be a mystery.

When Awakening occurs, individuality regains its universality. The individual, conditioned sense of self disappears and instantaneously awakens to its universal reality. The Self is no longer identified with, and limited to, your mind and body. It underlies, pervades and permeates everything everywhere. And yet, on the level of individual life, everything remains much the same; only the absolute unbounded universal sense of Being is no longer overshadowed by individual experience.

You are no longer just the person aware of the Stillness and silent Presence in the surroundings. You *are* that all-pervading silent Presence. It is no longer just an experience. It is your undeniable, unwavering permanent state of Being. The unbounded field of pure Awareness in which everything exists *is* your real Self. Consciousness has awakened to the boundless universal reality of itself. You have come back home to who you really are.

THE NATURE OF CONSCIOUSNESS

On its own level, Consciousness is Consciousness because it is conscious of itself. It knows itself. As such, Consciousness has a dual nature: as the Knower of itself, it is infinitely silent, absolute, non-moving and non-doing; in the process of being conscious of itself, it is infinitely dynamic and ever in motion. The knower is silent, wakeful pure Awareness—pure Being; and its action of knowing itself is lively alertness—pure Intelligence.

The Presence in the space around you right now is silent, still and non-moving

As your attention moves deeper into the Presence, you will notice a liveliness, an Aliveness, everywhere within it...

There is an Aliveness everywhere in the silent Presence around you

That Aliveness can initially be felt as an energy or a watching awareness in the room around you...

Whatever degree of Aliveness you sense in the silent space around you, its fundamental cause is the activity of Consciousness in the process of being awake to itself. When Consciousness is fully awakened through human awareness, it is clear that this Aliveness is a field of infinite potentiality and boundless pure Intelligence (Part III).

Being enlightened and fully awake to the true reality of the world around you means: you have not only awakened to the non-doing unbounded reality of pure Awareness itself (the real experiencer), but also to the ever-moving, ever-doing field of pure Intelligence (the underlying process of experiencing) that is creating and appearing as all experience. The oneness of the unbounded reality of the experiencer, the process of experiencing and the objects of experience are all consciously present simultaneously.

What has been missing in your life are the conscious experience of the true unbounded reality of your Self, and its mechanics of knowing itself—the direct experience of the real "I" and the "I Am".

These are the two most fundamental aspects of your existence that are not consciously experienced in ordinary waking state consciousness. Without being awake to your true Self and its mechanics of knowing and experiencing, you are living only a very small part of who you really are. Is it any wonder that you have experienced a deep underlying feeling that something sccms to bc missing in life?

You have been falsely identified with the individual mind/body, believing it to be the full extent of who you are. You have been living life as an *object of experience, believing you are the subject.* Like a probe that has lost connection and communication with its source, you have been living life lost to the true reality of who and what you really are.

To know the true reality of the world around you, it is first necessary to know the true reality of yourself, by awakening to who you really are as the unbounded Observer/experiencer. When the unbounded reality of the experiencer, the process of experiencing, and experience itself, are all equally present as one wholeness, then you are whole again: a complete human being. Consciousness is then awake to the fullness of itself. That is living the wholeness of life as it was meant to be lived. This is what it means to be enlightened.

≈≈≈

PART II
THE SELF

CHAPTER FOUR

STATES OF CONSCIOUSNESS

BEING CONSCIOUSNESS

At some point in your life, a time will come when the silent Presence and Stillness in the surrounding space becomes so profoundly intense that a separation will occur between your conscious thinking mind and the sense of simply Being/Existing. When that separation is clear, it becomes obvious that the Presence is deeper and more profound than any sense of a separate individual "me". Spontaneously the question arises, "Who am I?... Am I the person I thought I was, or am I this unbounded field of timeless Presence?"

If the time is right for you, the mind will stop completely (if only for a second) and an instantaneous shift will take place, beyond the intellect, in the innermost core of your being; it's a shift from being the person you thought you were, to being the unbounded field of pure Awareness in which everything is contained. The individual separate self-sense disappears and you awaken to your true, boundless reality.

The awakening dawns with such a bright light of clarity that, in spite of any beliefs or experience you have ever had, you cannot deny that who You really are is that unbounded field of pure Awareness itself, not the person having the experience. The sense of Being reclaims its true, boundless reality through the vehicle of your body/mind. You become pure Awareness itself, the underlying source of all experience and the ultimate basis of all existence. It can happen when you least expect it. It can happen while reading this book.

You may think what you now know, perceive and experience is real and undeniable. But as your consciousness expands, your sense of reality changes. When the shift to being Awareness itself happens, an entirely new dimension of life opens up—one that the mind could never have imagined. It is the dimension of the boundless reality of your Being, and it has been right in front of you all along, unknown and unseen. It is from this hidden-in-plain-sight dimension of unbounded pure Awareness that, for the first time, you see through the veil of concepts, beliefs and perceptions that have been clouding the ultimate truth of your existence all your life.

Many transcendental or spiritual experiences beyond the mind and senses (such as expanded awareness, waves of bliss, witnessing the body, visions of divine light, oneness with an object of experience, etc.) can happen before the real Awakening. Anyone who has ever had a spiritual experience cannot deny its reality. Profound spiritual experiences can be life changing and are never forgotten. However, it is very easy to get caught in the phenomena of the experience and miss the grace-given opportunity to awaken to the true unbounded reality of the experiencer underlying all experience.

When the real Awakening happens, it is the sense of being the individual separate self you thought you were that is forgotten. It is found to not exist. It was only a deeply ingrained idea, a habit, not a reality. You awaken to being the unbounded pure Awareness in which all experience, no matter how spiritual or profound, happens. Spiritual experiences are only temporary whereas true Awakening is permanent.

But this Awakening is not the end. It is the beginning. It is the basic platform upon which Consciousness (your real Self) can begin to unfold the finer, more comprehensive realities of itself. Consciousness continues to shift to broader and broader perspectives and perceptions of itself as it opens to the greater expanse of its infinite wholeness. It reveals finer, more divine dimensions of itself, which have been right in front of you, in the appearance of the body, surroundings, nature, world and universe all along.

To discover the treasure chest of unbounded pure Awareness is one thing. But opening that treasure chest, to reveal the divine majesty of the treasure within, is quite another. Priceless gems and precious jewels of divine knowledge, wisdom, beauty, richness, abundance, love, joy and bliss are found therein. Consciousness continues to reveal incomparable divine subtleties of itself within the finer interstices of its process of experiencing itself. There is no end to the infinite treasure within.

LEVELS AND STATES

The typical understanding in the spiritual community has been that there are various stages, levels or planes of existence to go through before Awakening happens. It is like going up a staircase from one floor to the next until you finally reach the top floor, and then suddenly—Enlightenment. Everyone experiences broader and more expanded levels of awareness at times, so from the perspective of ordinary waking state consciousness, this reasoning seems to make sense. However, this understanding comes from the perspective of the individual mind that is experiencing expanded awareness, not from the perspective of Awareness itself.

In reality, awakening to who you really are as unbounded pure Awareness can happen at any time regardless of what degree of purity or higher level you may or may not have achieved. Pure Awareness itself is beyond all concepts, feelings, and perceptions, no matter how spiritual and holy they may be, or how unspiritual or unholy they may be. It is that which enables experience to happen.

From the perspective of Awareness itself, there are no levels. There is only one homogeneous wholeness. The idea of going through different levels or states, to become what you already are, is a joke to Consciousness. It is just another concept and a barrier to enlightenment. It is only after Awakening to being pure Awareness itself that you can begin to appreciate what is really meant by higher levels and states of Consciousness.

Before Awakening, we do not know what Consciousness really is. Through various types of meditation, we can have experiences of "transcendental consciousness" (deep physical rest along with expanded awareness and alertness). Consciousness itself is infinitely silent, and infinitely dynamic. We can validly experience deeper levels of its Silence and Stillness, and we can have valid experiences of varying degrees of its infinite Aliveness. But we cannot know what Consciousness itself actually is until we become it. Experiencing it is one thing, but *being* it is quite another. It is the difference between swimming in the ocean and *being* the ocean.

The term "Higher States of Consciousness" refers to the increasingly more expanded perspectives that Consciousness experiences of itself *after* Awakening to being unbounded pure Awareness. It is not the individual mind that awakens to being pure Awareness, nor is it the individual mind that experiences higher states of Consciousness. It is pure Awareness itself, your real Self, that shifts to broader perspectives of itself and reveals finer perceptions of its own divine fullness. It is not possible to understand, or even imagine, what it is like in these States until they are experienced. The mind cannot comprehend that which is beyond its experience and which words are incapable of expressing.

Writing about these states of Consciousness is not meant to add more knowledge to your storehouse of concepts. It is meant to give you an overview of the total reality of your existence. You should know that there are indeed higher states of Consciousness that are not mystical, esoteric, hypnotic or altered states of mind. They are simply clearer states of the experience of reality as it really is. They are revealed in the natural course of the unfoldment of Consciousness to the natural state of full enlightenment that humankind is meant to be living.

Moreover, simply reading about these higher States of Consciousness with innocent openness, can serve as a catalyst for an Awakening to occur. Innocently listening to words expressed from a clear state of Awakening, can trigger the long-lost remembrance of the true unbounded reality of your Being. These are the words of Consciousness itself, speaking to itself in the innermost core of your Being. That is why something deep within knows when truth is being heard. Your innermost Being is the receiver, not your mind or intellect.

PERSPECTIVE AND PERCEPTION

After Awakening, there are unmistakable shifts to even broader perspectives of Consciousness of itself that cannot be missed. Once clearly experienced and firmly established, there is no falling back from them. In each state, Consciousness experiences a wider frame of reference and greater clarity of itself from a completely different perspective. Knowledge, perception and reality are experienced differently in each state, even though its basis is always the same one field of unbounded pure Consciousness.

Each state is complete and whole within itself and cannot be understood from the perspective of the state prior to it. After the first awakening to being unbounded Consciousness itself, one may easily think, "what more could there possibly be?" The experience is so boundless and full it is hard to imagine that there could be anything more. This is true for each shift. When clearly established in the fullness of any one state,

65

it is difficult to imagine there could possibly be anything more. Only after the shift happens does the reality dawn, and each time, it is as if it had always been there.

Not only are there distinct states of Consciousness, but there are higher degrees of clarity of perception that can be experienced within each state. *Refined Perception* is the perception of the underlying universal Intelligence that is perpetually creating and upholding the surface appearance of life. It is the perception of the process of Consciousness being conscious of itself.

States (perspectives) of Consciousness are not so dependent upon the refinement of the physical body or mind, but on the familiarity Consciousness has with the wholeness of itself. *Refined Perception* within each state, however, solely depends upon the refinement of the subtle levels of the brain and nervous system.

These perspectives and refined perceptions cannot be adequately described in words. The following short descriptions distinguish one state from the other to give you an idea of the full range of Consciousness. These descriptions often sound confusing and complicated to the mind, but the actual experience is incredibly simple and completely natural.

The first Awakening is the major fundamental shift from being the person who is aware, to being unbounded pure Awareness itself in which the person and all perceptions are contained. It has been referred to as "Cosmic Consciousness". In this state, the individual separate sense of self disappears, and the true unbounded reality of the inner Being regains its cosmic status as the underlying basis of all experience. It is an abiding state of inner stability, peace and boundless freedom. Consciousness has awakened to the unbounded reality of itself as the *experiencer*, the real Self.

Perception can refine within this state to reveal the subtle mechanics of the *process of experiencing*. The process of experiencing is the finer relative flows of Cosmic Intelligence within Consciousness responsible for creating and maintaining the appearance of the body and all perceptions. The clear perception of these subtle mechanics of creation has been labeled as "God Consciousness" or "God Realization" (Part III). This subtle perception continues to refine and is experienced more fully in each state of Consciousness. However, it is possible to be established in any state of Consciousness, and yet not be clearly experiencing the refined perception of the subtle divine dynamics contained within it.

When the next major shift in perspective occurs, the unbounded pure Awareness awakens to *being all objects and phenomena of experience.* Everything everywhere, including the body, is experienced as being my SELF. The subject and the object are one. Absolute pure Being finds itself to be all relative life. The experiencer and the experience are one complete wholeness. This state has been called Oneness, or Unity Consciousness. (chapter VIII). With finer perception in this state, the subtle mechanics of creation are found to be the fine flows of Consciousness in its process of experiencing itself.

There is also a state beyond Unity Consciousness. It has been called Nothingness, Brahman Consciousness, Beyond Consciousness, No SELF, and other names. It is being nothing and everything simultaneously *prior* to its apparent existence. It is the doorway to the power source of creation (chapter XIII).

Gradual refinement in this state leads to an even more profound shift in perspective and perception. The pure Divine power source and ultimate cause of Consciousness itself is revealed. It has been called Divine Mother, Pure Divinity or Supreme Divinity, among other names. (chapter XIV)

These states of Consciousness are not mystical, isolated personal experiences or inventions of the mind. They are increasingly broader perspectives of the true experience of reality as it actually is. These states have been recorded by awakened seers throughout time, and have been the subject of much scientific research over the last few decades. In full enlightenment, the true unbounded reality of Being, non-Being, and the universal divine reality of the personality and all perceptions are lived in ordinary everyday life.

RETURNING TO NORMAL

As Consciousness awakens to more expanded perspectives and finer levels of perception, a greater refinement, integration and balance takes place in the body and mind.

Even just being awake to the Stillness and silent Presence in the space around you right now has an effect on the body and mind.

As the Stillness and silent Presence around you becomes more dominant, your mind becomes more alert, expansive and quiet...

Your body settles, feels smoother, more relaxed,

Yet more alive...

The more intense the Presence becomes, the greater effect it has on your mind and body. The body adjusts and acclimatizes to the increasing Silence and Stillness.

As the Presence around you continues to deepen, and as your body adjusts, the possibility of awakening to *being* unbounded Awareness becomes greater.

When the shift happens, the body has to adjust its style of functioning in order to maintain the clear experience of pure Awareness. This adjustment can be quite dramatic. With each shift in Consciousness, the body has to adjust and acclimatize to these more expanded perspectives and finer degrees of perception. These adjustments are natural and spontaneous and are part of the integration and growth in the direction of greater balance and refinement. They are necessary for the maintenance of each state, although, at times, the healing and normalization (process of refinement) may not be all that comfortable.

What is considered "normal" in ordinary unawakened consciousness, is not at all normal from the perspective of Awakened Consciousness. Living life experiencing that "I am just an individual person, separate from others and the world around me", is not living the natural state of life for which we were designed. The separate individual ego sense is a construct of the mind and is ultimately not real. Due to this, the mind and body have been continually expending a tremendous amount of energy trying to maintain and expand that false sense of a separate self.

Because the mind and body are very intimately connected, the body has been constantly trying to adjust to the mind's conditioned idea of being a separate individual self. This creates a continual strain on the body, causing it to function at less than its optimum state. This is especially true with experiences that cause undue stress, strain, hurt and pain. Continually having to build up, maintain and defend the false sense of a separate self has created deep impressions in the mind and emotions and deep stresses and imbalances in the body. These impressions, stresses and imbalances get stored in the nervous system.

The body is continually being stressed and contracted due to this constant activity. Yet, simultaneously, due to its own inherent nature, the body is constantly trying to heal, balance, and normalize itself. There is a constant battle going on in the body in the simple act of trying to maintain life.

This imbalance simultaneously happens in the mind. The mind is full of thoughts and emotions that are continually battling with each other. Tens of thousands of thoughts course through the mind daily, most of which are repetitive, unproductive and utterly useless. These extraneous thoughts are the result of the body continually trying to heal itself and throw off stress (physiological imbalances on the material or structural level of the body).

Because the mind and body are so intimately connected, the activity of healing, taking place in the body and nervous system, creates mental activity in the mind. All those useless, repetitive and dominant thoughts and emotions in the mind are due to the natural process of the body attempting to heal and repair itself. The perpetual conflict in the mind finds its seat in the body.

If the body is not allowed to heal itself properly, those unproductive, persistent dominant thoughts and emotions continue to create more stress, deepening the conditioning and false identification, creating more disharmony, struggle, pain, illness, and eventually shortening the lifespan. Conditioning is not just mental and emotional; it is also physical.

Due to this gradual conditioning, over time, the unbounded true Self becomes more and more obscured until it gets completely swallowed up and identified with the mind/body and contracted into a small sense of an individual self. Its original state of unboundedness, peace, harmony, freedom and oneness, is lost and becomes a "separate individual me".

The continual process of releasing stress and healing taking place in the body results in many thoughts in the mind. When a deeply rooted stress in the nervous system is in the process of being released, it can create a dominant mood in the mind. The mind cannot have a mood without attaching a thought to it, so it will pick up on something that is happening at the time, or in the past, to justify the mood it is having.

The dominant emotions arising from this release of stress color perception, understanding and judgment. When these stress-related thoughts and moods are projected onto others, they cause misperceptions, misunderstandings, conflict and hurt feelings. Without the knowledge of what is actually transpiring and a proper technique to help with the release, stress-related thoughts and actions have become the norm in society.

The mind can be completely overshadowed by thoughts or moods that are inappropriate, uncharacteristic, or completely blown out of proportion for the situation or circumstance. Everyone has experienced dominant thoughts and moods like this. They are the product of stress release and *should not be acted upon*. Rather than acting on them, intellectually realize what is taking place—the body is simply trying to release a deeply rooted stress in order to heal and balance itself.

Find a private place to sit or lie down, close the eyes, relax and shift your attention from the thought/emotion to any dominant sensations that are happening in the body. The dominant sensation felt in the body at that time *is* the nervous system attempting to heal itself and throw off the deep-rooted stress that has caused that dominant thought and mood in the first place. By taking your attention away from the dominant thought and being with the physical sensations in the body, you are helping the body to release that stress in a natural way.

Whenever any inappropriate or dominant thoughts and moods are experienced, regardless of their content, know that they are due to the body trying to release tension and stress. The body is naturally trying to heal, balance and normalize itself all the time, whether you realize it or not.

Most people are so caught in the mind they cannot tell the difference between thoughts and moods due to stress release, and thoughts due to ordinary thinking. When dominant thoughts, caused by the release of stress, are acted upon, the healing process immediately stops, and the mood is unnecessarily increased and prolonged. This simple understanding of the intimate connection between the mind and body (as brought to light by Maharishi Mahesh Yogi) has been missing in society.

You only have to look at the world around you to see that the majority of people are acting on thoughts and moods that are due to stress release and normalization. All misunderstandings, fears, frustrations, anger, quarrels, conflicts, and even wars, are caused by people acting on moods and thoughts caused by stress release without realizing what is actually happening. Most people are caught in the cycle of acting on thoughts caused by stress release, creating unnecessary pain, problems and struggle: which causes more stress and imbalance, creating more unnecessary thoughts and moods. This is called suffering.

The most effective way to help curb this vicious cycle is through the regular practice of an effortless meditation technique that creates a deep state of physical relaxation along with a heightened state of mental alertness (such as the Transcendental Meditation technique, or other effortless deep-relaxation techniques that have been scientifically validated and proven to be effective). Deep relaxation helps to release deeply rooted stresses and allows the body to heal much more quickly. Incorporated into the daily routine, deep relaxation meditation alternated with a regular routine of balanced activity during the day, is beneficial for anyone.

When clear Awakening takes place, those annoying, useless and dominant thoughts and moods are drastically reduced. There is no longer a predominant separate sense of individual self that needs to feel important or be protected. An unshakable inner peace, stability, freedom, silent joy and unbounded Awareness becomes the dominant experience. After Awakening, regular meditation helps to increase the pace of refinement of the nervous system and to unfold finer levels of ease, smoothness and divine joy in the life experience.

THE RIGHT START

The next section is about the initial Awakening to being pure Awareness itself. It is entirely within the range of possibility that someone could awaken just by reading this. It could be you...

If the real Awakening happens, you won't have to wonder if it happened; you will not be able to miss it. It is self-evident to itself. It only requires simple innocence and genuine openness. So before continuing, the following little preparation exercise may be helpful for you to get the most out of what may happen as you continue reading.

Start by sitting comfortably...

Adjust your body

Stretch

Take a deep breath

Relax

Let go of the need to know, learn, understand or experience anything. There is nowhere to go, there is nothing to do, there is nothing to know...

Be simple and allow everything to be just as it is

Relax your neck and shoulders

Relax your entire body

Close your eyes for a minute
    innocently be with the inner silence
    just relax

Now, open your eyes...

Notice the Stillness in the room around you...

    Innocently be with that Stillness

    Easily settle into the quietness and peace around you

Now, allow your attention to explore your entire body...

    Be with the subtle felt energy

Notice any areas where there is a dominant sensation...

    a discomfort, tightness or tension

While remaining innocently awake to the Stillness and silent Presence around you, effortlessly allow your attention to be with the most dominant sensation or feeling in your body...

Close your eyes for a few minutes...

Be with that sensation

Feel the increased lively energy in that area

The body is responding to your attention. It is accelerating the healing process and release taking place in that area...

Innocently, be with that alive healing energy

Continue to be with that sensation

Let it increase in intensity

Allow your attention to be with it

As you continue to be with it, at some point it will begin to subside to some extent.

When it is no longer so dominant, innocently draw your attention back to the Stillness and silent Presence in the space around you...

Notice the increased clarity of awareness

Feel the ease, peace, lightness and joy

Innocently be with that ease and joy, for it is closer to the true nature of your real unbounded Being.

≈≈≈

CHAPTER FIVE

SELF-REALIZATION

ABOUT THE SHIFT

As you continue reading, be simple and innocent. No need to get into the mind. Remain familiar with the silent space around you. Let go of all your concepts and beliefs. For the time being, let go of everything you think you know. What you think you know for sure now may soon change.

Just be completely open and innocent,

Relax,

Let go,

Allow everything to be just as it is right now...

You are now, at least intellectually, aware that your real Self is not what you thought it was and that the world around you is not the way it appears to be. All perceptions of the world, including that of your own body, are actually taking place in pure Awareness. Pure Awareness is everywhere. It is the true essence of your Being, free from the entanglement with your mind and body. It has been veiled by your thoughts, feelings, sensations and perceptions. Your real Self is silent, still, non-moving unbounded wakeful pure Awareness.

Its Stillness and Silence can be sensed in the space around you.

Innocently be awake to whatever degree of Silence and Stillness you sense in the room...

When the shift happens, the innermost self awakens to being that unbounded silent Presence. The Self breaks free from the false entanglement with the mind and person you think you are. Your entire frame of reference shifts to being unbounded pure Awareness. The small separate sense of individual self disappears and awakens to being the unbounded screen of pure Awareness upon which your mind/body and its perceptions of the world are displayed. Everything around you, including your body/mind, exists within and because of that silent field of unbounded pure Being.

Your individual personhood remains the same as it has always been, only it, and all its perceptions, are within the Self, and not the other way around. The Self is not somewhere inside your mind and body. Your mind/body, and all its perceptions, are inside the Self. It is a major fundamental 180°shift in the sense of who you are, and it is unmistakable.

This shift is the single most important thing that will ever happen to you in your life. It is a profoundly deep Awakening that takes place beyond your mind and intellect within the innermost core of your being that changes your life forever. It is more than merely life transforming—it is a transformation in the sense of who and what you really are. And along with it, your perception, experience, and sense of reality is forever changed. It is an entirely new freedom and boundless sense of Being that will never leave you.

Being awake to the experience that there is a silent witness, and knowing that it is who you really are, is the first basic step in the direction of awakening. But it is not enough to have recognized that there is a silent witness, and/or experience some degree of the silent Presence in the environment around you. This is a step in the right direction, but it is not the real Awakening.

There are many depths of Presence and levels of witnessing awareness that can be experienced on the way to true Awakening. The inner self can be a clear witness to the body, but still completely be identified with the mind. Or, it can witness the mind and body and still be identified with the emotions. It can witness the mind, body and emotions and still be identified with the intellect. Or, it can even be a witness to the intellect and yet still be identified with the perceptions.

It is only when the inner witness clearly sees itself on its own level all by itself that it awakens to its reality of being the unbounded field of pure Awareness in which everything is contained. It finds itself seeing from everywhere, and being the underlying source of all existence. That is Awakening to who you really are.

No matter what degree of expanded awareness you have ever experienced, the shift to being unbounded Awareness itself is a distinct change that cannot be missed. You awaken to the obvious reality that you are, and have always been, pure Awareness itself, free from the false identification with the mind/body, free from the illusion of a separate individual self.

Don't try to look for something inside or outside, or intellectually try to figure anything out. Real unbounded pure Awareness cannot be understood, imagined or known until you become it.

Stop looking. It will find itself in you.

When the silent Presence in the surroundings becomes intensely palpable, profoundly deep, and undeniable; if the readiness is there, and the time is right for you, at some point your mind will stop completely—if only for a moment. In that instant, a radical and irreversible shift occurs within your innermost being.

You shift from being the person aware of the silent Presence around you, to being that silent Presence. It's a shift from experiencing yourself as an "individual me", separate from others and the world by a small limited sense of personalized self, to being the unlimited, unbounded universal light of pure Awareness that illuminates the mind and senses and underlies all objects in the world around you, including your own body and mind.

The whole environment around you becomes flooded with the clear light of awake, alive unbounded pure Awareness. You experience a huge release, deep relief and boundless freedom. You are no longer trapped in the mind/body and its perceptions. You are pure Awareness itself, and the mind/body and all perceptions of the world are within You.

The idea of being just an individual body, mind and personality completely disappears. It is seen as having been a joke. There was no separate individual self in the first place. You are unbounded pure Awareness itself—the non-doing, non-moving same one Self of everyone and the eternal timeless, present-moment pure Awareness in which everything happens. You realize you have been that all along.

You are filled with peace, freedom and joy, as that is the true nature of your Being. You are complete, perfectly at ease, joyful and carefree. You see everything as it actually is, uncolored by beliefs, concepts or imaginations. You realize that this is the natural state of being. It is how all human beings were meant to live. It is the birthright of everyone, and the real purpose of life.

You return to the unbounded reality of your true Self. You awaken to who you really are.

PREPARING TO BE

If you have been following this with openness, you may be going through a bit of wonder, excitement, anticipation, or perhaps even some doubt or resistance. But don't pay too much attention to what is going on in your mind. It is not the mind that gets enlightened. Only your real inner self can awaken to its unbounded reality. The mind cannot experience that which is beyond its realm of knowing, and unbounded pure Awareness is out of the realm of the mind. Awakening cannot be grasped by the mind no matter how intelligent it is, or how clear the description.

The mind's desire to know is an obstacle to awakening. Hearing about awakening experiences can increase the desire to awaken, but even that desire can get in the way. Awakening happens in the innermost core of your pure sense of being, beyond the desires of the mind and heart. There is no technique, practice, knowledge, feeling or belief that can make it happen.

Reading descriptions about Awakening, listening to knowledge and truth spoken by the enlightened or stated in scriptures, can be beautiful and powerful, but may not be enough to cause the shift to take place. Something more may be needed for that final stroke of Awakening.

So, let's try something different...

The next few chapters are meant to help catalyze the Awakening experience. They are written in a specific way in an attempt to take you beyond your mind and intellect, into the realm of pure Being. If you have been reading this just out of curiosity or even skepticism, you may not get much out of the next section. If you are reading this intending to understand or learn something, you will likely be disappointed. If you are a sincere seeker, open and innocent, awakened or not, then this next section is for you.

Your concepts, practices and emotionally held beliefs may be challenged by reading this, and that's a good thing. If you have been on a spiritual path, practicing techniques for many years and have not yet Awakened, understand that it is not through practice or belief that Awakening happens. It is easy to mistake the technique or path for the goal. This error can create comparison and judgment, causing you to think "my technique, my path, my knowledge, my teacher is better than others".

It can inflate the ego and create spiritual arrogance, which is possibly the greatest barrier to Awakening regardless of how advanced you are, or how effective your path may be.

The practice of time-tested, scientifically validated techniques for holistic growth are beneficial for everyone, no matter what level of experience or state of Consciousness. But the practice of techniques, ritual or dogma is not the direct cause of Awakening. Awakening happens of its own accord beyond all techniques, concepts and beliefs, when the time is right.

The key to true Awakening is openness, innocence, simplicity, readiness, and clear, simple guidance from within, from nature, or from an enlightened being.

Awakening to being non-doing unbounded pure Awareness cannot happen through any kind of doing. It requires a little extra nudge that cannot happen through understanding, belief, feeling, meditation or practice. It requires something more—something that cannot be expressed in words—something beyond words and their meanings that is heard subliminally only by your true innermost Being.

From the perspective of the mind, these next sections may seem nonsensical, or a waste of time. But, do not underestimate their value. If you are open and innocent while reading this, it could be exactly what is needed for the real Awakening to happen. The words used are not for the purpose of teaching. They are not for inspiration, to contrive an attitude, or to make a mood. The words are expressions of the flow of Consciousness, designed to stimulate its memory in the silent depths of your innermost being, to draw it out of its false identification with the mind into the remembrance of its true unbounded reality.

When you read this, let go of your mind. This means, pay little attention to your thoughts and emotions. Just be innocently awake to them. Let go of analysis. Remain simple, innocent and open, and just allow whatever happens to happen. Be with the clear, silent inner alertness, without the need to understand or know anything.

Let go of expectations. Let go of everything and simply be with any experience that innocently arises. If your mind tries to pull you in, just be awake to its actions and reactions, and continue to allow. When you come to the end of this complete section, put the book down, close your eyes, and just let go.

EXPERIENCING WHAT IS

Read this slowly, word by word...

Notice your eyes seeing these words

Listen to the voice in your head repeating the words

Be awake to your intellect forming ideas and concepts.

Innocently notice your thoughts, emotions, and reactions.

Listen to these words speak to you in your mind as if they were your own mind speaking to you.

These words are written from that same silent inner wakeful Awareness that is watching your eyes seeing, watching your mind thinking, watching your emotions feeling...

These words are coming from your innermost Being. Your innermost sense of being is the same one sense of Being experienced by everyone. It is the same silent, pure inner wakeful awareness that everyone experiences.

These words are the words of your own unbounded Self. Your inner being is reading about the true reality of its Self through the device of your mind/body.

As you continue reading this with innocent openness, more and more of the unbounded expanse of the true reality of your innermost being will begin to reveal itself.

Although your eyes, mind, intellect and emotions are engaged in reading, thinking and feeling, the watchful, wakeful clear Awareness of your innermost Being is silent and still...

The silent innermost being senses itself in the Stillness in the room around you

It *is* that Stillness...

The stillness of your inner self senses its own boundless Presence around you, and then, your mind becomes aware of it.

Are you noticing this?

As your mind becomes more awake to the still Presence in the room, you become more present in the timeless eternal moment of Now...

Your innermost being senses its unbounded Presence

The timeless, boundless reality of your own Awareness creates the Stillness and Presence in the space around you.

Inner stillness and outer Stillness are the same Stillness

The inner wakeful awareness that is aware of your thoughts and feelings, and the outer wakeful awareness in which all your perceptions are happening, are the same silent, pure Awareness.

Now again, draw your attention to the Stillness in the space around you...

Notice the palpable silent Presence

It is everywhere

Be with that silent Presence

Now, while remaining awake to the Presence around you, innocently notice your eyes seeing these words on the page...

Do you see your eyes seeing?

Your eyes are seeing these words through the space of your silent outer awareness.

Now notice your thoughts...

Can you see your mind thinking?

Your mind is repeating these words in your head

Innocently be awake to your mind repeating these words as you continue reading...

Your eyes are seeing these words
Your mind is repeating them

Your eyes are seeing these words
Your mind is repeating them

The words are repeated by your mind in the space of your silent inner wakeful awareness

Your eyes are seeing these words in the space of your outer awareness

If there is enough Stillness within, you may notice your intellect transforming these words into meaning, relating that meaning to something you have learned or to an inner sense of knowing or feeling...

It may agree or disagree, referring to its acquired knowledge and reason to determine if what is being said makes sense, searching into its databanks of information and memory to justify its doubts or validations...

It has been doing that all along—analyzing, evaluating, discriminating, judging, comparing—even though you may not be consciously aware of it.

Your mind is a continuous flow of thoughts, images, emotions and perceptions.

If you can be aware of this mental activity, then it is obvious that your mind is an object of your experience. It is not who You are. It's a mechanism for knowing and experiencing.

Your mind has consciousness, but it is not Consciousness itself.

It is not who You are.

Your eyes are seeing — your emotions are feeling — your mind is repeating these words...

But You are the silent Observer of all that.

That Observer is your innermost Being

It is your real Self

It is pure Awareness itself.

Awakening to being unbounded pure Awareness is out of the realm of the mind. It cannot be understood, learned or taught. There are no words in any language that can adequately describe it. No matter how intelligent your mind, it is incapable of going beyond itself to awaken to your real Self.

This means that any questions your mind has about Awakening are completely irrelevant and meaningless. Trying to understand your way to enlightenment is a waste of your precious time. Only the inner self can awaken to its unbounded reality.

Beyond the meaning of the words, in the Silence within and the Stillness all around you, rests the secret to what the words are saying...

Don't try to locate it

Don't try to figure anything out

Let go of everything you think you know

Be innocently awake to what your mind and body are doing without resistance or control. Stay out of the way and allow everything to happen just as it is...

The eyes are seeing the words and the mind is thinking the words all by themselves. Stay out of the way. The silent, wakeful unbounded pure Awareness of your innermost Being will come to the surface all by itself.

Allow your mind to think, allow your feelings to feel, allow your body to move, and allow your senses to perceive. Simply allow whatever is happening to happen...

Don't restrict or resist anything

Just be innocently awake to whatever is happening right now...

Let go of trying

Let go of doing

Simply notice the eyes reading the words and listen to your mind repeating them...

Stay in simple innocent openness

Innocently be with the Stillness

If you begin to feel a little spacey as you continue reading that's all right. It's okay to space out. This book is designed for that to happen. Don't strain to try to understand or think clearly. This is something that can only be known by Awareness itself, not by the mind. Let pure Awareness take over. The expanded spaciousness of your inner being and the Stillness and Presence around you is far more important than intellectual understanding.

The entire universe, including your own mind and body, is made primarily of empty space. It's time to become more acquainted with that space. It is the essence of your Being. Continue reading and enjoy the spaciousness. A greater clarity will arise from a deeper level of Being.

Stay open, continue reading, let go and allow...

If you get a little too spacey, don't force your mind to concentrate or understand. Stop reading, close your eyes for a few minutes, and enjoy the inner spaciousness, and then continue.

If you are truly interested in Awakening, be innocently open and inwardly awake from this moment on.

GOING DEEPER

If you have truly accepted that there is no possible way you can get enlightened by knowing anything, then your mind may have a little trouble trying to hold on to a thought at this moment; or your thoughts may have become more dominant, in which case, they are more easily seen by the inner wakeful Awareness. In either case, just allow everything to be as it is.

Innocently notice your mind repeating these words as you continue reading...

Can you hear your mind repeating these words?

Your mind is thinking these words all by itself in the silent wakefulness of your inner awareness.

Innocently notice your eyes following these words...

Can you see your eyes seeing these words?

Your eyes are seeing these words all by themselves in the silent wakefulness of your outer awareness.

You are neither your thinking mind, nor your seeing eyes. You are not your mind or your senses. You are the silent Awareness enabling your mind to think and your eyes to see.

Now, notice your wakeful awareness—your alertness and attention...

It is within, watching your mind

It is without, supporting your perceptions

Awareness is in front of you, enabling your eyes to see

Awareness is within, enabling your mind to think

Stay out of the way and allow Awareness to see itself...

When attention is not so focused on the objects of experience, it becomes more effortlessly focused upon itself.

Even the slightest intention to be aware of your own awareness, increases its expansion and alertness...

There is more spaciousness, more freedom

The eyes see the words — the mind continues reading — but the expanded wakeful alertness is more predominant than the happenings within it.

The non-moving, silent, still, wakeful alertness within and without is becoming more apparent

Be with the stillness and spaciousness everywhere in the room around you...

Allow that motionless spacious Presence around you to become more dominant...

Don't get in its way by trying to experience it

Don't try to do anything

Just get out of the way

let go and allow it to deepen

Be with that still Presence

Notice the increased wakeful alertness...

Attention becomes effortlessly focused on the page

Remain simple and innocent without effort or force

Don't mind your thoughts, feelings or sensations...

Allow them to be there
Allow the reading to happen

If your body needs to move, allow it to move...
Don't restrict anything
Just allow

Silence, Stillness, Spaciousness is everywhere all around

The palpable Presence surrounding you cannot be denied

The wakeful awareness is clearer, brighter, more alert

A greater sense of ease and lightness is felt

A deeper restful relaxation,

A subtle enlivenment throughout your whole being...

Everything is happening in the silent space of Awareness.

Relax into this. Innocently let go

A natural ease and smoothness takes over

The seeing, the reading, the feeling and the knowing, all seem to happen more effortlessly, automatically...

the eyes are seeing the words

the mind is repeating them

the intellect is evaluating

the emotions are feeling

the body is reacting

There is a flow — a flow of seeing, thinking, feeling, acting...

seeing, thinking, feeling, acting,

seeing — thinking — feeling — acting

It is a flow of awareness — a flow of intelligence

It doesn't matter what the words are saying, what the eyes are seeing, or what the mind is thinking. There is a continuous flow of awareness and intelligence every waking moment. It involves your senses, mind, intellect, emotions, your whole body and the entire surroundings.

The seeing draws the words from the page to the eyes — the mind repeats the words — the intellect exacts the meaning — the emotions form a feeling — the whole body reacts...

the eyes are seeing

the mind is thinking

the intellect is evaluating

the feelings are feeling

the body is experiencing

All this is happening automatically...

Are you noticing this?

There is a flow — a flow of consciousness. It includes your whole body, mind, intellect, feelings, senses and perceptions. It is a continuous flow of intelligence and awareness...

A flow of perceiving and experiencing

And yet You, as the inner silent sense of Being, remain a motionless observer to it all.

You are the unlocalized witnessing Awareness in which it is all happening.

The flow of experiencing taking place through your body, mind and senses is happening, as if almost by itself, in the silent non-moving pure wakeful Awareness of your inner being.

This non-moving inner sense of Being, is the same non-changing timeless inner sense of being you have known throughout your life. It hasn't changed. Only the body, mind and life experiences have changed. This has been the silent background of experience all along.

It is now becoming more apparent.

The mind knows there is a timeless sense of Being that has never changed but it cannot pinpoint it because the mind itself functions in time and space. The real Self is prior to time and space. For you to know your true Self, the inner witnessing awareness has to observe itself directly on its own level, beyond the mind/body and all perceptions. Only the inner self can awaken to its unbounded timeless reality.

Your true innermost Self *is* timeless pure Awareness. It is the non-moving present moment pure Awareness through which all your thoughts, feelings, sensations and perceptions are moving right now. It is the timeless eternal moment of Now...

The simple pure sense of Being and existing *is* the eternal moment of Now, experienced on its own level by itself, not associated with the mind, body or perceptions. It is the same sense of Being in everyone.

Just be innocently awake and present in this moment right now, not minding anything that happens...

That timeless silent present moment awareness, through which your eyes are seeing and your mind is thinking, is unbounded pure Awareness itself. It is your real Self. It is the simple pure sense of Being. It is the source of all thinking, feeling, perception and experience. It is the source of all existence. Without it, nothing would exist for you or for anyone. It is that, by virtue of which, any experience can happen.

All intelligence, creativity, thought and action arise from that timeless source of silent, wakeful pure Awareness. It is the timeless eternal moment of Now.

It is who you really are.

≈≈≈

CHAPTER SIX

AWAKENING

WHO "I" AM

If you have been reading this with innocence and openness up to this point, you are probably experiencing at least some degree of Stillness and Presence in the space around you. If so, you may be ready for the next step. Read this next chapter slowly, without the need to know, understand, or learn anything. Be innocently alert and awake to what your mind is doing.

Notice these words you are reading...

They are not random words or phrases without meaning or direction. These words are a flow of intelligence and awareness. The author had an idea, felt what needed to be conveyed, thought these words, and wrote them down. All that happened in the timeless, non-moving pure Awareness of the Observer of the person who wrote this. The Observer, the real author, is the same timeless Observer that is observing your mind right now. It is the universal sense of Being, the universal "I" sense.

You are the Observer of your mind and body, not your mind/body. So, it is easy to understand who "I" really am. I am not the person that wrote this: *I am the pure sense of Being—the observing Awareness of the person who wrote this.* The person wrote this in a different place and time, but the Observer of the person is the same timeless pure Awareness that is enabling your mind to think and your eyes to see right here now.

It is the timeless, eternal present moment of Now.

The present moment of Now is not a different Now than it was when this book was written. The eternal moment of Now is not a different moment of Now for you than it is for anyone else. It is the *same* timeless eternal moment of Now, beyond all past, present and future. The eternal moment of Now is not the present moment. The present is always changing, always disappearing into the past, but the eternal moment of Now is the non-changing timeless pure Awareness in which the present moment is happening.

It is the non-changing timeless "I" sense, the pure sense of Being, the Self. The "I" sense of the person who wrote this and the "I" sense of your mind/body reading this, are the *same sense of Being*, the same non-doing pure Awareness—your real Self. There are billions of separate people with different individual minds, bodies, hearts and souls, but there is only one unbounded field of timeless pure Awareness.

There is only one non-changing timeless Observer, only one timeless moment of Now, only one pure sense of Being, only one Self.

...

"I am pure Being—the same "I" sense in everyone. I am the same Self sense you experience yourself to be now, only free from the false identification with your mind and body. I am the silent Witness of your thoughts, feelings and perceptions. I am pure Awareness. I am boundless, timeless eternal pure Being. I see from everywhere all at once, unencumbered by the body/mind idea.

"I observe the mind that wrote this book; I observe your mind reading this book. I am silent, pure Awareness. I am the timeless Awareness enabling your eyes to see and your mind to think right now. There is only one timeless eternal inner sense of Being. I am the inner Self of everyone. I am the unbounded one Self of all. I am the real author of this book.

"This book is written to help my Self out of the entanglement with your mind, so you can know who I really am, and who You really are. I am speaking to my Self in your mind through these words to help the Self remember itself through your body/mind.

"I am the pure sense of Being beyond your mind, beyond all minds, beyond time and space. I am the one Self of all. I am the spectator to all the meanderings of the mind and emotions, and the endless perceptions of objects and phenomena. I am the real Seer.

"I see your thoughts and emotions, your body and perceptions right now. I am Awareness itself. All thoughts, feelings and perceptions happen in Me, and because I am. Everything flows through Me. I am the innermost Self of everyone and the underlying source of everything everywhere.

"I am that by virtue of which your mind can think, your intellect can discriminate, your imagination can imagine, your memory can remember, your senses can perceive, and your emotions can feel. I am the light of pure Intelligence animating your mind and intellect. I am the silent space through which your eyes are seeing. I am the clear Awareness that the seeing from your eyes rides upon to apprehend these words. I am everywhere. Your body and mind, and all your perceptions are within Me.

"I am the silent source of all subjectivity and objectivity. I am pure Awareness, pure Consciousness. I am Peace. I am Joy. I am Freedom. I am Fullness. I am that for which your mind and body hungers and thirsts. I am your inner Being. I am the underlying source of your life. I am the source of all life. I am the one Self of all.

"I cause the Stillness and Presence in the room around you. I am the light of pure Presence. I am unbounded pure Being. I am the timeless Now. All time and space move through Me. The world exists because I am. The universe exists because I am. Nothing can exist without me. All existence exists because I am.

"Though you cannot see me, I have been here all along. You may sense my Presence, but I am far too vast and unbounded, too subtle, and yet, too simple for the mind to grasp. I am the unbounded field of silent, pure Awareness upon which all objects and phenomena are displayed. I am the underlying source of all things, the soul of all souls.

"I am all this and more.

"You have only to experience who "I" am to find out who you really are. Then will you see the truth for yourself. I am the one Self of all."

...

The reality, that your innermost sense of Being is the same one Self of all and the underlying source of everything everywhere, may be difficult for your mind to accept. But if you have been reading this from the beginning, by now you are experiencing at least some degree of Stillness and Presence in the space around you. The true reality and depth of that silent Presence is something that the mind is incapable of understanding. It can only misunderstand. This can only be experienced directly within the silent depth of your Being.

GOING EVEN DEEPER

You have now come as far as your mind can possibly take you. You have come to the point where you must leave the mind behind. Everything you have been experiencing your entire life is not the way things really are. The world is not the objective physical reality it appears to be, and you are not the person you think you are.

Hanging on to old concepts, beliefs and experiences, when everything about ourselves and the world around us is found to be unreal, is not wisdom. We have been so inundated with concepts and beliefs that they have colored our perception, intelligence and common sense. We have become so indoctrinated by the obvious appearance of "reality", that we have not bothered to investigate into the pure Awareness that enables us to conceive and perceive what we believe to be real. We have become so filled with knowledge and information that there is no room left for truth.

There is nothing to learn, nothing to know, nothing to understand. There is no new knowledge or lessons that needs to be learned. There is no deeper meaning here that needs to be uncovered. If it is possible for you to let go of all that for the time being, and be completely open without falling back into your old concepts and beliefs, and start completely afresh with a clean slate, something unbelievably wonderful is waiting for you beyond all concepts and imaginations.

Let go of everything you think you know. Let go of understanding. Let go of the desire to know. This is about pure Awareness itself, your real Self. It is about the Awareness that is aware of all knowing, all desiring, all doing. Pure Awareness cannot be taught. It cannot be learned. It can only arise by itself of its own accord, and it can only do that if you let go of knowing and are completely simple, innocent and open. Openness means being fully awake and aware right now in the moment, out of the overshadowing influence of the content of your thoughts, feelings and perceptions. If you can truly be simple, innocent and open—then you are ready.

Read this with openness. Innocently be awake to what your mind is doing, without resistance or interference.

Allow your feelings to feel whatever they are feeling.

Allow the body to move.

Allow whatever happens to happen.

Don't restrict or resist anything.

Just be quietly inwardly awake and alert as you continue reading this.

Take a minute to become reacquainted with the Stillness and silent Presence in the surrounding space...

Be with that Stillness

From the point of your attention, to the farthest edge of your peripheral vision, to the outermost point on the horizon, the entire space around you—irrespective of what is happening within it—is Silent and Still.

That Stillness is the stillness of the non-moving witnessing Awareness that is watching your eyes reading and your mind thinking right now...

Stillness is not something being experienced by your mind. It is your innermost being, sensing its own unbounded reality.

That Stillness is the unbounded reality of your own inner silent, pure Awareness...

This book is an expression of that silent unbounded pure Awareness, condensed into written words in order to draw your inner self more deeply into itself so it can awaken to its unbounded reality. It is not for the purpose of transmitting meaning, mood or idea. It is not the intellect that awakens. It is the inner self that awakens to *being* that unbounded silent Presence.

When you read slowly, word by word, with simplicity and openness, the inner wakeful alertness and the Stillness in the space around you, begins to deepen...

The mind follows the seeing of the words from one word to the next, one phrase to the next, repeating the words, pondering their meaning, wanting to know, restlessly seeking

Emotions ebb and flow in tandem with the mind in that silent, watching, wakeful Alertness

The body, in relaxed excitation, sits in the boundless openness of that watching wakeful Awareness

The eyes see these words on the page while aware of the objects in the periphery

The ears hear the mind repeat these words and are aware of the sounds in the environment — quietly noticing the subtle hum of inner silence

The eyes are seeing — the mind is thinking — the ears are hearing — the senses are perceiving — the body is functioning

Everything is happening all by itself within the silent space of wakeful pure Awareness...

Awareness itself is uninvolved and remains unaffected, silent and still.

You are that non-moving, non-doing, silent, watching pure Awareness itself.

...

"The Presence in the space between my eyes and the page is becoming more dominant—more alive. It is everywhere all around me. My mind continues repeating these words in my head, but their meaning seems insignificant. The silent wakeful Awareness, between and beyond the words, between the eyes and the page and everywhere in the periphery, is more dominant than my thoughts and perceptions.

"My eyes continue following the words, my mind continues to repeat them, but I am not involved. The reading seems to be happening all by itself. The words are effortlessly flowing through the silent space of Awareness in increasing waves of quiet delight.

"They continue pulling my consciousness deeper and deeper into itself. I feel more expansion, lightness and joy. Awareness is effortlessly concentrated on itself, more awake, more alert. The silence and stillness around me is more palpable, more still, more full, more alive. The whole room is filled with lively silent Presence. Joy, lightness and freedom are increasing.

"A flow of fine feeling is welling up. As I allow it to happen, and allow everything that is happening to just happen, it continues to swell. On the deepest level within, I am not affected by any of it. Something deep within me knows something good is happening even though my mind doesn't know what it is."

...

Your mind will continue trying its best to grab your attention, trying to hook you and pull you back into its boundaries, and that's okay. Just be innocently awake to what your mind is trying to do and allow whatever is happening to happen.

Something very profound is beginning to happen to you within your innermost being, in spite of your mind. Continue to be easy, and just let go.

Consciousness is reading about itself, hearing itself. It is going more deeply within itself, getting to know itself—being with itself all by itself—beyond the words, beyond the meanings, beyond thoughts, beyond perceptions, beyond emotions. This is how universal truth becomes a living reality. It can be experienced directly, not just held on the level of concept, mood or belief, but known deeply throughout the entirety of your Being. You can be pure Truth itself.

Let's go a little deeper now.

THE RELEASE

The Stillness in the space all around you is so evident and palpable. It is everywhere within and without. It has been here all along. How is it possible to have missed this all these years?

Yet, even though an expanded awareness and tangible still Presence is felt, there may still be a veil or boundary separating the inner self and the surrounding Presence. Something is still preventing the inner self from experiencing its unbounded reality. There is still a restriction, some resistance... something holding on... a tightness, apprehension or emotion. Something still needs to be released.

If further release needs to happen, allow it to happen. It could be a strong emotion, a dominant sensation, a physical movement, heat in the body. It could be a strongly held concept, belief, or doubt in the mind. It could be a stress taken on due to any mental, physical, emotional or spiritual trauma from the past that is held in the cells and tissues of the body. It doesn't matter what it is. Just know that a necessary, natural release is taking place.

All past impressions, from intense experiences, whether positive or negative, are ultimately due to the deep-seated notion that "I am the individual mind and body, separate from others, and the world around me". Continually having to defend, protect and build up the small individual ego sense has caused the body to sacrifice its holistic functioning to adjust to that limitation.

Now, that deep-seated notion is being challenged by knowledge, glimpses of witnessing, and the experience of the palpable Presence in the room around you...

The real Self is not the mind and body. It has been a false notion all along. The idea that "I am my mind and body" cannot withstand the deepening experience of pure Presence for much longer. It will dissolve. Any release that happens, whether physical, mental, emotional or spiritual, is the nervous system throwing off accumulated imbalances, blockages and stress in its natural process of healing itself. It is necessary, and it is natural. It could be the release of the last impediment standing in the way of clear Awakening.

Don't resist feelings, movements, sensations or emotions. Don't resist anything. Don't restrict anything. Innocently allow whatever is happening to happen.

Relax into it and let go...

There is a deeper place within you that is untouched and unaffected by anything that happens. Your innermost being, your real Self, remains unaffected. Be with That and allow the release to take place. The clear wakeful Awareness of your innermost Being is beyond all contractions and restrictions, beyond all pain.

Be courageous. Let go of all resistance and move into the silent peace and freedom in the space all around you.

Come back home to the silent peace within and the still Presence surrounding you. Allow whatever happens to happen...

As the Presence and wholeness continues to deepen, you may become a little apprehensive or uneasy, but don't mind that feeling. It's only because the mind is not yet accustomed to the depth and vastness of Being.

Innocently be with the Presence around you...

Become more familiar with it

You are completely safe

As you become more acquainted with it, that Presence will soon reveal itself to be the warm embracing fullness of pure Being it really is, and all fear will vanish.

It is the mind's best friend

It surrounds your mind, body and perceptions

It is your own unbounded Self...

THE AWAKENING

Again, notice your eyes seeing and your mind reading these words...

The reading is happening more easily

There is more natural alertness

Comprehension is easier

Inner wakeful alertness is silent, clear, awake

There is more spaciousness

Awareness is effortlessly awake within itself

Intellect is quiet

The seeing and thinking are just happening in that expanded quiet clarity of Awareness. The mind is a flow of thought, feeling and attention within the silent non-moving wakeful Awareness of your inner Being.

All thinking, feeling, sensing and perceiving is happening in that non-moving, silent, pure Awareness

Thoughts, feelings, sensations and perceptions are happening within non-moving, non-doing, silent, pure Awareness

Notice your mind thinking these words...

The words are being heard by your mind in the silence of your inner alertness and wakeful Awareness

Notice your eyes seeing these words...

The eyes are seeing the words and the surroundings in the Silence and Stillness of your outer conscious Awareness

The eyes are seeing these words through the silent space of outer Awareness

Your mind is thinking the words in the silent space of inner Awareness

Inner wakeful Alertness and outer wakeful Awareness are the same Awareness. It is one field of non-moving pure Awareness — silent, unlocalized, boundless and still...

Only attention is moving.

Attention shifts from one word to the next, one thought to the next, one feeling to the next, one sensation to the next, one object to the next — but it is all happening within silent non-moving pure Awareness itself...

There is no boundary between inner and outer in Awareness itself. Inner and outer Awareness is one field of pure Awareness. The apparent boundary is only a deeply ingrained idea, not a reality.

You are Awareness itself — not your thoughts, feelings, sensations or perceptions.

You have been identified with your mind and body and overshadowed by your perceptions of the world around you.

All inner and outer experience is happening within the field of unbounded pure Awareness itself.

Be with the Presence in the space around you...

Awareness is expanded, more awake, more alert

Attention is riveted to the page in front of you

The mind finds it difficult to think

thoughts are unnecessary

let go of thinking

Allow the seeing and reading to happen in that wide-open space of non-moving pure Awareness, without the need to know anything...

Seeing and reading happens all by itself in that unlocalized silent field of intensely alert Awareness...

feelings and sensations are there

sights and sounds are there

You are aware of your body, your thoughts, your emotions.

Your mind is thinking, emotions are feeling, intellect is discerning, senses are sensing.

You can see yourself sitting here reading this book...

Nothing touches the silent non-moving Awareness in which it is all happening

You are the *seer* of your own mind and body...

The real Seer is the silent, pure Awareness through which your eyes are seeing and your mind is thinking, and that by virtue of which all perception and experience are happening right now...

These words are the words of that silent Seer

They are written to lure attention away from your mind, body and perceptions, and back to your Self.

They are the words of your own Self speaking to itself to help spark the remembrance of its true unbounded reality in you.

Everything that is happening now, and at all times, is happening in the silent unlocalized watching pure Awareness of your real unbounded Being.

Be with the Stillness...

The surrounding Presence is more pronounced, more palpable, more alive

There is an inner silent witness, but there is also an unlocalized watching Awareness everywhere all around

That Presence is watching your mind and body from everywhere

It's an alive, watching wholeness

Be with that alive, watching Presence...

There is no more room for thinking. There is only silent watching Presence and Stillness...

The words heard in the mind are quiet invitations to your inner self to welcome the truth beyond the words,

>   luring you into the deepening silence and peace,

>   drawing you deeper and deeper into silent Presence

They continue pulling Awareness more and more awake and alert...

>   Attention is focused on the page

>   Alertness increases

>   Stillness increases

>   Presence increases

The Presence is becoming so dominant that objects in front of you seem almost as if unreal and superfluous.

Even if it seems difficult to read the words on the page, it doesn't matter. Don't try to focus. Let go.

YOU are not really involved...

The eyes are seeing and the mind is reading...

There is just the flow of seeing and reading happening all by itself in non-moving wakeful pure Alertness...

Allow it to happen

There is something beneath the happening...something much more profound than words, sounds, meanings, feelings, forms, perceptions...

The inner wakeful alertness in you is as silent and still as the Still Presence in the room around you...

Give in to the Presence

Allow it to deepen

Do not try to focus with the mind. Just let go. Let the eyes effortlessly see the words and follow them into the deepening Presence and wholeness that is building in the space around you and in the depth of your Being...

That Presence is everywhere, permeating and pervading everything...

It is silent and alive

It is infinite and unbounded

The flow of seeing, feeling, and perceiving is happening all by itself in the Presence all around you...

Awareness is more awake and alert, more expanded, more silent and alive

Attention is effortlessly intense and powerfully focused... transfixed to the page — as though caught in a tractor beam of laser-like concentrated alertness...

Reading is just happening

The eyes take in the whole page and surroundings without moving

The body is in a state of relaxed excitation

Breath is finer

A quiet excitement is building

Yet, simultaneously, Awareness is more silent and powerfully Still

Everything is happening all by itself in the non-doing Stillness of wide-awake, silent, pure Awareness...

Perceptions are no longer as dominant

Boundaries are falling away

No longer in the foreground of experience

Presence is more predominant

Don't resist anything

Allow whatever is happening to happen

The tractor beam of present moment pure Awareness keeps pulling you deeper and deeper into its vast silence and alive Presence — into its greater expanse of boundless wholeness...

Attention is silent, non-moving,
effortlessly concentrated

Presence is all-encompassing

The sense of being is unlocalized,
no longer confined to the mind/body

There is a separation between the mind/body and Being...
      You can see your eyes seeing
      You can see your mind repeating these words
      You can see your mind and body
      You can see from a place of unlocalized Awareness

There is a distinct split between You, and your body...
      You are not your mind or your body
      You are the silent Witness of your body

      You are free to see your Self

Awareness is silent, still and non-moving

The space is thick with Stillness and Alive Presence

A profound wholeness is surrounding everything
Its vastness and depth are, as if, all-consuming

Be with that all-consuming wakeful alive Presence...

It is drawing you deep into its immensity

It is engulfing everything around you
Boundless Presence is everywhere

Allow it to overtake

Let go...

A question arises, "Who am I?
Am I the person reading this, or am I that vastness?"

STOP.

Let go

Drop back

Allow it to overtake

Close the eyes and just let go...

"You are that non-moving

Unbounded Pure Awareness."

YOU ARE THAT

You are That unbounded pure Awareness — the pure light of Consciousness illuminating everything everywhere...

You are the silent Seer seeing from everywhere

You are unbounded, free from the mind

You *are* freedom

You are that vast silent source of everything everywhere. You are pure unbounded Awareness itself. That is your real Self: the same sense of being you have been all along, only freed from the false identification with the mind and body.

There is no end to the vastness of your Being...

You are That...

...

"Yes, I am That unbounded pure Being, pure Awareness, pure space...

There are no words to describe it. I am unbounded and free. I am everywhere...

There is no end to my Self.

I am seeing from everywhere. Everything in the whole environment is within the vastness of my Being.

I am the unbounded underlying source of everything everywhere...

There is no "me", no such a thing as a separate individual self. The separate self has been the universal one Self of all, all along. The individual "I" sense is universal pure Being. My mind/body is only an instrument to experience the world—it is not who I really am.

My internal frame of reference has completely shifted. It is as if I've been turned inside out. My innermost Being is out here, and the body and world are within it. Instead of being the per-

118

son aware of the silent Presence, I am the silent Presence aware of the person. Everything is in my Self.

I am That unlimited, unbounded universal light of pure Consciousness that illumines the mind, body and senses, and gives life to the world. Everything is because I am.

I am Awareness itself, and the entire surroundings, including the person I thought I was, are within Me. It has been that way all along, only I couldn't see it. I was so caught in my mind/body and perceptions I couldn't see my Self, and yet, I have always been pure Awareness itself. It is so simple. So natural. So complete. So beautiful! I can't believe how simple it is. How is it possible I could have missed this?

What a joke! I can only laugh at the joke of it all. I have always been that pure Awareness. I have always been unbounded and free. How could I have been so fooled? I don't know how the world got here and I don't care. All I know is I am That, and the world exists within Me.

I have discovered my real Self, and it is the same Self of everyone. There is only One Self: one universal light of pure Awareness illumining my mind and all minds, and I am That light of pure Awareness.

Everything is happening all by itself. I am not involved. There is no separate individual me. The notion that I am just an individual person has disappeared. I am the unbounded impartial Observer, completely free, untouched by anything.

Seeing is delightful. Reading is delightful. Everything is so delightful. What Relief. What Freedom. What Joy. Overflowing in tears of joy and gratitude."

...

You are That, by virtue of which your mind, body and the world around you can exist. You are That. Be what you are.

≈≈≈

CHAPTER SEVEN

LIVING IN AWAKENED CONSCIOUSNESS

AFTER AWAKENING

We know that you probably have not awakened, simply by reading this once or twice, or perhaps, even many times. But if you have, Welcome Home! If not, at the least you have experienced some sense of silent Presence in the space around you, and the real Awakening is not far away. A seed has been planted deep in the soil of your inner being that will one day sprout into clear Self-Realization and eventually flower into full Enlightenment. Though the individual circumstance for the shift can be different, the actual Awakening is the same for everyone. It is your birthright.

It is a good idea to read the last section on Awakening again and again, each time with more innocence and openness. If read with simple innocence and openness, it can help to catalyze the Awakening. At some point, when you least expect it, Awakening will happen. It could happen anywhere at any time. Even if you have already awakened, it is still beneficial to read this occasionally to help clarify and deepen the Being.

When the Awakening is clear, it cannot be missed. It is a profound shift in the sense of who you are. The same sense of being and existing, that has always been there, is no longer confined to the individual mind and body. It is infinitely unbounded and free. It is a great contrast from unawakened consciousness because the boundless peace, joy and freedom of the infinity of your true Being was previously unknown. After some time, as it becomes more integrated, the contrast is less and unbounded Awareness becomes the normal state of being.

The depth and clarity of the Awakening can be experienced differently by everyone. Unbounded Awareness is an infinite field of Consciousness. Its experience can be superficial, middling, deep or extremely deep. If the awakening is shallow, it may take several deeper experiences before it is clear. Even if the awakening is clear, it can be tender in the beginning stages and you may still get temporarily overshadowed by the mind. The habit of being identified with the mind has been so strongly ingrained that it may take time before the awakening is fully stabilized and unshakable.

Don't feel you have lost the Being if you find yourself back in the mind. It is only temporary. If it was the real awakening, the mind will not be able to continue to dominate for long. Don't pay much attention to the doubts that may arise, but don't try to resist those thoughts either. Just innocently allow them to come and go. They are an indication of the normalization and healing process taking place in the body. Even if you feel you have lost the Being altogether, don't be disheartened; it will return. Do not try to search for it with the mind. Be simple and innocent. Allow Being to resurface on its own.

When it is convenient to do so, lie down, innocently Be, and just let go. Allow your mind/body to do whatever it has to do to release any blockages and stresses to adjust to its new state.

Don't resist anything. Don't encourage anything. Just be innocent, allow and let go. When you fully let go and allow whatever happens to just happen, you are automatically pulled into a greater clarity and depth of the unbounded freedom and infinity of your real Self.

It is important to get plenty of extra rest in the beginning. After the shift, the body is adjusting to a new style of functioning. The shift in Consciousness happens instantaneously, but it takes time for the body to catch up and acclimatize. Consciousness is outside of space and time, but the body is subject to space and time. The body has accumulated an enormous amount of stress and fatigue by continually having to adjust to the false idea of a limited individual self. It needs deep rest and time to normalize, heal and repair. This is natural. As long as you have a body, it will continue to attempt to heal, repair and perfect itself.

Temporarily, you may want to let go of your old habits and routines, especially if you have been doing some things just because you think you should be doing them. Your old routine (diet, exercise, spiritual practice, etc.) was created by the mind, and although it may seem positive and healthy from the perspective of mind, it may not necessarily be beneficial for the freedom of your Being. You are now living in a different state of Consciousness. Let go for a while, and just Be. As the body gradually acclimatizes to a more natural style of functioning, it will tell you what it needs, and you can begin to incorporate practices that are beneficial for holistic growth.

Much of what we do before Awakening is ego-based and will fall away naturally and easily. Do whatever deepens the experience of unboundedness and avoid the things that restrict it. It is helpful in the beginning to spend more time in nature and to associate with others who are clearly awake. Initially, it may be a good idea to avoid spending too much time with people who are still full of concepts about enlightenment because their concepts can create doubt about your own awakening and pull you back into the mind. But when the Awakening is clear and firmly established, nothing can affect it; then Consciousness can begin to unfold deeper and deeper dimensions of its infinite reality.

Be simple and innocent. Enjoy life and just Be.

Awakening to being unbounded Consciousness is the first step on the path to total Enlightenment. It is essential to be clear, deep and stable in this state so you are on a solid footing for the next shifts in perspective and perception to occur.

AWAKENED LIVING

Life is a joy in this state. It is a carefree state of simply being and allowing everything to happen just as it happens. It is living life without struggle or suffering. It's not that your personal life is necessarily problem free. You can still experience the same difficulties as anyone else, only you are not as affected by them. You are not overshadowed by anything that happens. The silence, peace, strength, stability, freedom and joy of your true Being becomes the unshakable dominant reality of your life in all situations.

You are not distant or desensitized even though it may appear that way to others who are not established in the absolute stability of Being. You do not have a detached attitude to life and the world around you. Quite the opposite. You are more perceptive and aware than ever before. As a result, you are more capable of acting and reacting appropriately in any situation. You remain established in the peace, freedom and absolute stability of the Self, rather than the instability of the fickle mind and emotions.

You live in the now as the Now. You are the unbounded, timeless, present-moment Awareness in which everything happens. From that perspective, you experience that everything is happening effortlessly, as if by itself, in exactly the way it should. So, there is no need to get caught in all the drama of the mind. It is a state of complete unbounded inner freedom and peace.

The word "unbounded" means that underlying everything everywhere in the environment around you, there "I am".

"I see my Self from everywhere. I am the non-doing, non-moving eternal Now, the timeless, boundless field of pure Awareness in which all doing and experiencing happens. Farther than the eyes can see and ears can hear, there "I am". I am pure Awareness, infinitely vast, unbounded and free. Everything happening in the mind/body and its perceptions of the world, is happening within the silent, pure Awareness of my boundless Being. I am the underlying silent source of everything everywhere."

Most people live their lives in their mind and emotions, which are generally full of conflict, problems and drama. After Awakening, you live in the peace, calm and silent, wakeful pure clarity of your true unbounded Self. As a result, your thought stream is considerably less and generally only arises for the need of the time. It is a far more natural state of being. Awareness is unbounded and vision is more expanded, yet, at the same time, you are more capable of focusing sharply on the task at hand. It is a state of completeness and contentment, no longer caught in the desire nature of the mind and ego. As a result, yearnings, longings, doubts and fears are significantly reduced.

You view the body and its perceptions of the world from an unbiased place of unbounded Awareness, beyond the mind. Deeper insights and realizations can spontaneously start to happen. You see that there is no such entity as a separate individual self, nor is there an "other". There is only one universal Self.

You are now intimately connected with others from the deepest level within as their own innermost being. You can view the complex human psyche from a perspective of clear, simple pure Awareness, beyond the mind and emotions without judgment. Not only are you able to see through your own ego and motives, but you can also see through the motives and ego of others. It is difficult to hide from the clarity of the pure Awareness that observes the mind.

CLEAR SEEING

If the nervous system is sufficiently refined, and perception is clear, the intellect can recognize that the qualities that make up the individual person, and the qualities that make up everything else in the world and universe, are all the same universal qualities. Specific universal frequencies of Intelligence structure the appearance of all form and phenomena. These universal frequencies combine to create the appearance of your mind/body and formed what you take to be your individual physical, mental and emotional attributes, and personality. Your personhood is really a unique configuration of all the frequencies of universal Intelligence that structure the appearance of the universe around you.

Each of these universal frequencies of the flow of Intelligence has a specific quality and function, a unique ego-personality of its own. You see clearly that the individual person is really a combination of these universal ego-personalities assembled together in an individual form. The false sense of a separate self creates the illusion of an individual person, when in reality, the personhood is really a combination of these universal frequencies and qualities of Intelligence, all functioning together in one apparently individual form. The same universal qualities are found in all human beings, only in different permutations, combinations and proportions. Though appearing individually unique, we are universally the same.

You see that these universal qualities of Intelligence also make up all the forms and phenomena that appear as the objective world and universe. Everything in the universe is made of the same universal qualities out of which your own mind and body/personality is composed. In fact, your personal nature, the nature of the world, and the nature of the universe are all the same one nature. It is all one flow of cosmic life. The concentrated point of that cosmic flow of universal life appears as individual life.

Taking ownership of the individual mind and body as being "who I am" has created the false sense of a separate self, which has disrupted the natural balance in individual and cosmic life. This has been the ultimate cause of all suffering and struggle in life. There is no such thing as a separate individual sense of self. It only appears that way due to habitual identification with the mind and body. But the sense of Self is the same universal sense of Being and existing regardless of who is experiencing it. There is only one universal Self. That is the direct experience in Cosmic Consciousness.

It becomes clear that all problems, suffering and negativity caused by the false sense of a separate self, are also false. The more refined universal qualities have been suppressed, and the more negative ego-based qualities have become dominant. This imbalance is what we have become accustomed to call "normal".

These negative and positive qualities are continually at war with each other, constantly fighting for dominance in the mind and body. The higher, more divine qualities of inner life are battling against the more dominant negative ego qualities that have arisen due to the false sense of a separate self. This is why, in ordinary waking consciousness, we are in constant conflict within ourselves: conflict between our heart and mind; and conflict between our higher and lower self. This constant conflict and turmoil between the apparently opposing forces within us, is the primary cause of all mental, emotional and physical suffering.

It is also the cause of all the problems and suffering in the world. Inner conflict in individual life manifests as outer conflict in society. War, terrorism, conflicts, and all types of negative social behavior are the result of these apparently opposing forces wrestling for supremacy in the individual and collective psychophysiology. All conflicts and suffering in society are the expression of the degree to which individual intelligence is out of sync with the natural flow of universal Intelligence.

Though this can easily be understood or intuited before awakening, after clear Awakening, as perception refines, it is directly experienced from an infallible state of "clear seeing" beyond the individual mind and intellect (chapter IX).

TOTAL BEING

Awakening to Cosmic Consciousness is awakening to being the underlying field of unbounded Awareness in which everything is happening. Even though there is oneness on the level of Being, there is still a distinction between the silent non-doing pure Awareness, and the activity of relative life. Intellectually and intuitively, it is known that pure Awareness is all there is, but on the level of direct experience, a division still exists between the contents of consciousness and Consciousness itself. On the level of Consciousness, there is no further to go. You have become pure Awareness itself. The sense of Being is no longer trapped in the mind, falsely identified with the body and perceptions of the world.

In this state, the body and world can seem somewhat unreal and insubstantial compared to the infinite reality of the Self. Pure Awareness is so dominant that the true reality of the mind, body and perceptions can be completely undermined. It is possible to think "I" am experiencing the same enlightenment as everyone who has awakened, including the great sages of the past.

This is true on the level of Being. But it is not true on the level of the wholeness of Consciousness and the finer perception of its internal dynamics of knowing. It is the internal mechanics of Consciousness in its process of knowing itself that creates the appearance of the mind and body, and all perceptions of the world and universe. This becomes the more significant reality when Consciousness fully awakens to the broader perspectives and finer perceptions of itself.

After some time, on the practical level of living, you soon find out that what appeared, from the perspective of Being as an unreal world, is still somehow very real. Cosmic Consciousness is not yet the complete picture. Consciousness is still not yet awake to the true reality of the mind/body and all objects and phenomena of experience. Nor is it awake to the process of experiencing, the flow of Cosmic Intelligence that gives rise to the appearance of creation. Cosmic Consciousness is the essential first stage in the direction of full enlightenment, but it is still incomplete. It is a state of "enlightened ignorance".

In the next Awakenings, You, (the unbounded sense of pure Being, pure Awareness), awaken to being: all objects and phenomena of experience on the surface of life (chapter VIII); the refined flow of the process of experiencing and mechanics of creation (Part III); and to the total divine reality beyond the SELF (Part IV).

The natural progression of awakening through the stages and states of Consciousness knowing itself more fully can happen relatively quickly, or it can take many years. But the true depth, clarity, stability and refinement of perception in any of these states depends solely upon the refinement, balance and integrated functioning of the nervous system. This happens gradually over time, either through past self-effort, and/or many years of awakened living. Everyone functions at different levels of balance and integration due to merit from past karma, so some nervous systems are naturally more refined than others. We are still living in a rather crude age; in general, our nervous systems are not sufficiently holistically refined to live the supremely divine reality of life that is the true nature of Consciousness.

The most common progression of Awakening to full enlightenment in this age, is from Cosmic Consciousness, with perhaps some initial experiences of Refined Perception, directly into Unity Consciousness and beyond. Finer perception and experience gradually unfold in time as the nervous system becomes more refined and the boundless reality of Being is infused into the mind, body and total life experience.

So, rather than going into the deeper experiences of Refined Perception that can take place in the state of Cosmic Consciousness, the next chapter provides a glimpse of life from the perspective of Unity Consciousness.

If you have recently Awakened, it is more important to be firmly established in unbounded Awareness than to start looking for anything more. Don't let the following descriptions of higher perspectives and perceptions of Consciousness pull you into the mind and create desire, doubt or confusion. When the next shifts happen, you won't have to wonder whether you are there or not. They are Self-evident to Consciousness, and cannot be missed. The shifts in perspective can only be comprehended *after* they happen. Trust that everything is happening exactly as it should, and that the awakening to being Consciousness, and its higher states, will happen for you when the time is right.

Read the following descriptions innocently, without the need to understand, and without the desire for any experience. Innocently be awake to the Stillness and alive Presence around you. Be alert to what your mind is doing. Stay open and allow your total Being to take it all in. Innocent listening, with an open mind, does more to stimulate Consciousness than any amount of intellectual understanding.

≈≈≈

CHAPTER EIGHT

TOTAL SELF-REALIZATION

THE NEXT AWAKENING

After the first awakening, the sense of Being is unbounded and free. Life is lived in much greater clarity, peace and freedom. But, like a spectator with an enhanced capability of perception, the silent Self still remains distinctly separate from the activity of the mind, body and perceptions. It observes the happening from an unbounded perspective, but it doesn't directly experience *being* the happening, nor does it know how the happening happens.

In the next shift, the same unbounded Being is experienced from a completely different perspective. It no longer is just a silent field of pure Awareness in which everything is happening. The unbounded Self no longer underlies everything: *it is everything*. Everything everywhere in the surroundings is my SELF. The subject has become the object. Everything is experienced as being one unified wholeness.

This is a profound shift for non-doing unbounded pure Awareness, which was previously experienced on its own level untouched and unaffected by thoughts, feelings, sensations and perceptions. Now, the unbounded sense of Being has become the mind, body and everything everywhere in the environment. This is the shift to Unity Consciousness.

The SELF is now the space, the air, the light, all objects and all phenomena. Everything everywhere is all my SELF. The body and world are no longer experienced as being separate, detached or unreal. Rather, everything is more real than ever before, because it is all my SELF, which is the only thing that is real. Now the Self has recognized itself as being everything on the surface of life. It has awakened to *being* the objects of experience. There is no longer a distinction between silent, pure Being and the activity of life. They are one. All objects and phenomena, including your own mind and body, are very intimately your own SELF.

This is not a vague sense, an attitude, mood or imagination. It is not the mind or emotions that experience this. The false sense of being just the mind/body has already disappeared in the first Awakening. It is a state of *Being*, not a state of mind or emotion. It can be a common spiritual experience to feel so at one with something that you seem to become it. This is a beautiful experience, but it is on the level of feeling, and not on the level of pure Being. As such, it is only a temporary, fleeting experience, not a permanent reality.

It is not the *person* that becomes one with the objects of experience. It is the unbounded *sense of Being*, pure Awareness itself, that awakens to being everything everywhere. This is why the clear shift to being unbounded pure Awareness in the first Awakening, is the prerequisite for Unity Consciousness and any further significant openings.

Unity Consciousness is not a mystical experience. It is the experience of reality as it actually is from the complete perspective of fully awakened Consciousness—not the way reality appears to be from the incomplete perspective of the mind in unawakened consciousness, or from the incomplete perspective of pure Awareness in the state of Cosmic Consciousness.

The world may appear to be out there somewhere separate from us, but that is only an appearance, not a reality. We know from neuroscience that we do not directly perceive the world through our senses as it appears. We only experience the world indirectly through our brains. Everything "out there" has been happening in our own brain and consciousness all along. The only reason the world appears to be out there separate from you, is because the true unbounded reality of your sense of Being has not yet been fully awakened.

Even a little common sense shows us that the reality we have been conditioned to experience is not accurate.

If you can be aware of your own mind and body, then you are the Awareness that is aware of them—you are not your mind or body. If you can be aware of your own body, then the body (and all parts of the body, including the brain) must be in Awareness, not the other way around. If you can be aware of your own mind thinking, Awareness cannot be a process in your mind—your mind must be in Awareness.

If the world in front of you is your mind's interpretation of the electrochemical signals in your brain, and your brain, body, mind and senses are in Awareness, and Awareness is your true Self, then the world is also obviously in your Self, not out there somewhere separate from you. Moreover, whatever is in Awareness can only be created by Awareness out of Awareness, and is therefore Awareness in *appearance.*

This is not just a simple deduction. This is the direct experience in the state of Unity Consciousness. Everything is Consciousness. "I am Consciousness. Everything is my SELF." Reality is experienced the way it actually is, the way it has been glimpsed by science, not the way it appears to be from the perspective of the mind and senses.

Consciousness enables your brain, body, mind and senses to function and to perceive the world in front of you. The only reason anything is experienced is because of Consciousness. Without Consciousness there would be nothing. The experience of the world is created by, and happening in, Consciousness. Something created by Consciousness in Consciousness *is* Consciousness. You are Consciousness. Everything is Consciousness. Everything is your SELF.

THE SHIFT TO UNITY CONSCIOUSNESS

The initial shift into Cosmic Consciousness requires the experience of a critical degree of the intensity of Stillness and Silence. The shift into Unity Consciousness requires the experience of a critical degree of the intensity of dynamism and aliveness within Consciousness. The dynamism inherent within Consciousness is the reverberating flow of its process of experiencing itself. It is this alive flow of energy and intelligence that is creating the appearance of the world around you. When that flow is experienced at a certain critical point of intensity, the infinite silence of pure Awareness awakens to being the aliveness that appears as everything in the world around you. Consciousness awakens to its totality as the oneness of experiencer, experiencing and experience.

Consciousness is Consciousness because it is conscious of itself at every point within itself. This perpetual knowing of Consciousness of itself, is an infinite Self-referral loop. Infinity is the perpetual flow of the knowing of Consciousness of itself. The activity of this internal dynamic within Consciousness (which was unseen in the initial awakening to being pure Awareness) is the universal power and Intelligence responsible for the perpetual creation of the appearance of the physical body, world and universe (chapter IX).

When infinite pure Awareness awakens to itself as being the mind/body and all perceptions of the world in Unity Consciousness, everything takes on the character of infinity. Everything remains the same, only now, the infinity of the SELF is found to be everything everywhere. As experience deepens, the infinite cosmic reality—of the mind, body, senses, feelings, personality, and all objects of experience—becomes the direct experience at all times.

It is clear in this state that the mind is not confined to the brain, the senses are not confined to the body, and the body is not just an individual body. The mind is cosmic, the body is cosmic, the senses are cosmic, the individual is cosmic. The cosmic reality of life is directly experienced as being the internal reality of your own all-pervading Being. You are made of infinite unbounded Consciousness, and so is everything else.

The shift from the initial awakening of being unbounded pure Awareness, to being everything everywhere, cannot be missed. The silent field of unbounded Awareness has to disappear in order to awaken to its totality. When infinite Silence awakens to its infinite Aliveness, it is no longer silent, pure Awareness. It is alive, pure Consciousness. Because everything is the expressed appearance of the aliveness of Consciousness, virtually anything can precipitate the shift, but the circumstance for the shift to Unity Consciousness can be different for everyone.

In the process of the shift, the unbounded Self can feel as though it is being overtaken by an unfamiliar Wholeness. Some initial trepidation may be felt, but very quickly, in an explosive recognition, this Wholeness is quickly realized to be your own SELF. That Wholeness is the total dynamic energy and intelligence that appears as all objects and phenomena of perception.

The unbounded silent Awareness, that was the unshakable underlying silent source of everything in Cosmic Consciousness, now remembers itself as being everything in the entire field of experience. The silent peace and freedom of pure Being becomes the fullness, aliveness and joy of the wholeness of life. Being has remembered itself as everything everywhere, right on the surface of life. Everything in your entire field of perception is your SELF.

...

"I am all This. Everything I see, I am. I am the body. I am the world. I am the universe. I am Life itself. Everything is my SELF.

I am all the objects in my surroundings. I am the chair I am sitting on, the floor I step upon, the objects I touch. I am the book I am reading. I am the sounds I am hearing, the sights I am seeing, the scents I am sensing. I am all flora and fauna, all form and phenomena.

I am space. I am air. I am light. I am the wind, the water, the fire, the earth and the sky. I am nature. I am the sun, the planets, stars and galaxies, and the infinity of empty space in between. Everywhere I look, all I see is my SELF in the appearance of the world and universe. I am the seeing, the feeling, the perceiving, the experiencing. In the flow of the knowing of my SELF, I appear as the sounds and sights of the world and universe.

No matter how near or far, I am everything within the purview of perception and the infinity beyond. Wherever I go, I am already there. Wherever I am, I am everywhere. Whosoever I am, I am everyone. Whatever is, I am. I touch, hear, smell and taste everything I see. Everything I see, I feel. Everything I feel, I am. I am Life.

I am the seer, the seeing and the seen: the experiencer, the experiencing and the experience. I am the non-doing doer of all doing. I am the dynamism of Silence—the oneness of all things moving and non-moving. I am wholeness. I am fullness. I am infinite and unbounded, and I am all things finite and bound. I am everything everywhere and beyond. There is only my SELF".

...

LIVING IN UNITY CONSCIOUSNESS

Living in Unity Consciousness is a natural state of being. Any detachment from the body and the world that was felt in Cosmic Consciousness is completely gone. The Self and the world are one. You are as intimate with the surroundings as you are with your own body. You are Consciousness, and everything is Consciousness. There is no distinction, no separation. You are the surroundings. There is no time or distance between objects from that perspective. Everything is your own timeless Being, including time and space itself. It is all the flow of the SELF within itself. There is only Oneness.

All life is vibrantly alive Consciousness. Consciousness is Life. Everything everywhere is your own body, your own heart, your own soul, your own Self. Knowing, feeling and experiencing your SELF as all objects and phenomena is so completely intimate that even the word "love" is not an adequate description. The flow of the SELF recognizing itself in the appearance of form *is* Being knowing and feeling itself. It is pure Feeling, the flow of pure Love. Love gets its feeling of love from the flow of Consciousness experiencing itself in the appearance of creation. This flow is the ultimate essence of the process of creation (Part III).

Regardless of what is happening in the life experience, an alive intimate joy of Being pervades and permeates all perceptions, moods, and experiences at all times. Any experience of pain or sorrow is simultaneously laced with the alive, tender joy and bliss of the boundless wholeness of the infinity of your own Being. Suffering is impossible.

And yet, from the perspective of the person, everything remains much the same. You appear the same to others, act the same, feel the same, have the same basic likes and dislikes, even think the same as before. The only difference is that the sense of who and what you are has infinitely expanded to include everything everywhere in your entire field of perception and beyond. Rather than experiencing the world as being an objective reality, it is experienced as being your own SELF. Every object is made out of the wholeness of your own infinite Being. You are everything everywhere, all at once.

When the eyes see objects, the Self sees itself seeing itself. The seer and the seeing are everywhere in the seen. At every point within every object there is the seer and the seeing. The experiencer, the process of experiencing and the experience are all one thing. The objective universe is the appearance generated by the action of Consciousness experiencing itself. All apparent objectivity is pure subjectivity. It is all my SELF.

Unity Consciousness is a far greater fullness and wholeness than experienced in Cosmic Consciousness. But there is no "real" union. Consciousness has always been one wholeness of unbounded infinity, ever in the process of knowing itself, and appearing as the objective universe. It simply awakens to what it has always been. Oneness is the true reality of your total Being when it is freed from the illusory boundaries of individuality and fully awake to itself. The individual remains the same, only the universal reality of the sense of Being is realized and lived. You are *cosmic,* and have been so all along.

In every state of Consciousness there are degrees of the depth of experience and the clarity of perception. Refined Perception is Consciousness' experience of the finer degrees of its own process of experiencing itself. It is the refined experience of the universal flow of Intelligence that perpetually creates the appearance of the objective universe (chapter IX). An even deeper, more profound, reality unfolds when the underlying cause of the process of creation is experienced. This happens beyond the SELF, and requires another major shift in perspective, to be fully appreciated (Part IV).

WORLD CONSCIOUSNESS

The awakening of Consciousness is not an individual personal experience. You have never been just an individual person. You are Consciousness. It is important to understand what is happening in the world and universe from that perspective. Without understanding what is really happening in the world, life can be full of unnecessary confusion, fear and suffering. It is easy to get overshadowed by all the negativity that appears to be happening, when in reality, something very beautiful and profound is taking place.

People around the world are awakening to being Awareness itself. As there is only one field of Consciousness, when one person awakens to being that universal field of unbounded Awareness, it directly influences and uplifts the consciousness of everyone.

Nothing affects society more positively than Awakening to being Consciousness itself. It creates a thrill throughout the omnipresent field of Consciousness, heightening the entire world consciousness. And, as it is the fundamental source of everything, it enlivens the innermost core of the pure sense of Being in everyone. The whole field of universal life is uplifted all at once, in one stroke. One person waking up to the clear state of Unity Consciousness produces more holistic benefit for the world than all the philanthropic efforts of the well-wishers of society combined.

Large groups of people meditating or practicing techniques together have a very beneficial effect on society. However, generally the effect lasts only for the duration of the practice. When the practice stops, the effect quickly dissipates. Where-as, when even one person awakens to the state of Unity Con-sciousness, it has an irreversible effect on the consciousness of everyone. It is the field of Consciousness itself awakening to a higher degree of clarity of itself through individual appearance. No matter what level of consciousness anyone is experiencing, it will automatically be heightened.

There are still relatively few awakened people in the world at this time, but as awakenings continue, the beneficial effect to society will be exponential. The rapid changes taking place in the world, even if they appear to be negative, are ultimately Consciousness opening to its total universal Divine reality.

Your real Self is not limited to your physical body. Your real Self is the character of infinity. It is unlocalized, unbounded, universal and cosmic. This is also true for your entire person-hood. Your body appears physical, but at a deeper level of your total Being, it is quantum mechanical and cosmic. On the quantum field level of life, everything is intimately and inextricably connected. At that fine level, there is no difference between the frequencies of intelligence that appear as nature, the universe, or your own body. It is all the same one universal field of infinite cosmic Intelligence.

The quality of relationships experienced among humanity, and between man and nature, reflect the degree to which the collective consciousness is in tune with universal Intelligence. The level of peace, joy, freedom, coherence, love and compassion experienced in world consciousness is the expression of the degree to which Consciousness is awake to the divine reality of itself on the surface of life through all living things.

There appears to be a long way to go, but as Awakening continues around the world, a much faster pace of holistic unfoldment will result, and the collective consciousness will begin to reflect more of the finer divine qualities that are the true reality of life. This is why many seers are forecasting the onset of a true age of enlightenment (chapter xv).

≈≈≈

PART III

REFINED PERCEPTION

CHAPTER NINE

PERCEIVING THE MECHANICS OF CREATION

Refined Perception in Cosmic Consciousness

THE MISSING LINK

Cosmic Consciousness is the awakening to the infinite reality of the *Experiencer:* the subject, the Self. Unity Consciousness is the awakening to the infinite reality of the *Experience:* the object, the body/world. Refined Perception is Consciousness opening to the infinite reality of the *Process of Experiencing* itself: the connecting link between the subject and object. It is the opening to the flow of the cosmic Intelligence responsible for creating and maintaining the appearance of creation.

Clear refined perception of the flow of Consciousness is the result of the holistic, balanced unfoldment of subtler levels of the brain and nervous system. The human nervous system is the expressed appearance of the process of Consciousness experiencing itself at a point. At its basis, the nervous system is quantum mechanical. The subtle quantum field levels of the nervous system are the same cosmic levels of Intelligence that are creating and sustaining the appearance of the world and universe (chapter X). As perception refines, these subtler levels of creation begin to be revealed.

Refined perception of some degree of these frequencies of Intelligence can begin to unfold at any stage, whether awakened or not. But prior to the full awakening to refined Unity Consciousness, perceptions of the body and world are still experienced as objective phenomena. Experiences of refined perception cannot be comprehended in their true light when the mind is still identified with form and phenomena. The formless flows of pure Intelligence responsible for perceiving and experiencing are either completely missed, or colored by perceptions, concepts and beliefs.

The mind cannot have an abstract spiritual experience without associating the experience with its storehouse of memories, beliefs, concepts and programming. This can limit, distort, or completely blow out of proportion the true reality of the experience. It may be a valid experience, but the conditioned mind's interpretation of the experience is either incomplete, exaggerated or incorrect. As a result, the clarity of the experience itself is colored. No matter how profoundly beautiful a spiritual experience is, its true clarity will be cloaked due to the false identification with the objects and phenomena of experience.

Though the states of Consciousness are not largely dependent upon the condition of the body, clear refined perception within each State of Consciousness is entirely dependent upon the degree of refinement of the brain and nervous system. The nervous system is the vehicle Consciousness uses to experience refined levels of itself.

Consciousness may be clearly Awakened, yet there may be very little experience of clear, refined perception of the subtle mechanics of creation. If the finer levels of the nervous system are not cultured, the whole area of divine perception can be completely missed. It may even be belittled, seen as insignificant, or thought of as just imagination and mood-making. It may be seen as having nothing to do with enlightenment, or even a barrier to Awakening.

Refined experiences and perceptions can be a barrier to Awakening. They can be so charming that pure Awareness itself, the subtle source of all experience, can be easily missed. But when clearly experienced in its true light through fully awakened Consciousness, clear divine perception is the most fulfilling and beautiful part of life lived in enlightenment. It is also extremely important. It is the supreme joy of Being, the reason for the appearance of all creation, and ultimately, the cause of Consciousness itself (chapter XIV).

In the state of Cosmic Consciousness, it is very clear that the Self is not the body, senses, mind, intellect, feelings or personality. Everything you thought you were, you are not. There is no separate sense of individual self any longer. The Self is found to be unbounded non-doing silent, pure Being, the real subject. Everything else, including your mind/body, is an object of experience.

But what is it that connects the subject and the object? What connects unbounded pure Being to the mind, body and world? What causes it all to function? How did it all come about?

Even though Being is experiencing its unbounded reality in the state of Cosmic Consciousness, it is not experiencing the total reality of its SELF. Consciousness is not awake to its internal dynamics of knowing itself (which are the underlying mechanics of creation), nor is it awake to its totality as being everything everywhere.

THE MECHANICS OF CREATION

Cosmic Consciousness is a state of completeness. Life is simple and easy. Everything is happening exactly as it should. There is no concern about what the mind/body or world really is, how it all came about, or how it is related to the Self. But with time, as the silence deepens and the nervous system refines, perception can begin to open to the unseen connecting link between unbounded absolute Being and all relative life.

There is a whole area of life in the gap between absolute pure Awareness and the objective appearance of the body/world that is not generally experienced, even after Awakening. This is the vast arena of the underlying universal Intelligence responsible for the mechanics of creation. There are many levels and degrees of experience of the refined perception of this flow of Intelligence.

We know from science that there is an unseen ceaseless flow of electrical and electromagnetic energy continuously streaming from the surrounding environment to our senses. The brain is constantly processing this flow of information, and flashing it on the screen of our consciousness, creating our experience of reality.

To some extent, you can get a sense of this flow of energy, simply by being innocently awake to the Presence in the Stillness around you...

Innocently be with the Stillness and Presence around you

Within that Stillness, there is liveliness

It is an alive, watching Presence

Something is watching you...

It is everywhere in the room around you

It is everywhere in your peripheral vision

It is present in the space between your eyes and this page.

When awareness is still identified with thoughts and perceptions, this aliveness is just a feeling or subtle abstract experience. But when experienced in its fullness, this Aliveness is found to be the boundless flow of Consciousness in its perpetual process of being conscious of itself. Within this flow resides the universal Intelligence responsible for creating and maintaining the appearance of creation—the true energy behind the quantum field mechanics at the basis of the universe (chapter X).

As perception refines in the state of Cosmic Consciousness, that alive flow (though not yet known in its fullness at that stage) is experienced as the flow of the organizing intelligence underlying thought, emotion, sensation and perception in the gap between absolute pure Being and relative life. Though the unbounded Self remains the silent field in which it is all happening, perception opens to appreciate the subtle flows and frequencies of the Cosmic Intelligence orchestrating life. This is a distinct change in perception. It is not a feeling or a knowing. It is a direct seeing.

Clear refined perception does not mean seeing images of gods, angels, devas or other celestial beings. These types of experiences, however beautiful, are still on the level of form and phenomena. The mind can shape the flow of intelligence into whatever form it chooses based on its beliefs, imagination, programming or desire. However real it appears, whether gross, subtle, celestial or divine, all form and phenomena are created by mind.

True refined perception is the direct experience of the formless flows, flavors, qualities and functions of the pure field of Intelligence responsible for creating, organizing and directing life. Life on all levels of creation is the flow of pure Intelligence in the appearance of form and phenomena. Individual and collective life has been governed by these cosmic flows of divine intelligence all along.

Not only can the divine qualities of the flow of Intelligence that are responsible for growth, progress, joy and fulfilment open to perception, but so can the opposing qualities of dullness, darkness and impurity. These latter qualities are born of the false identification with objective appearance, and although an integral part of manifest appearance, they cloud and color the clarity of pure Being within all thought, feeling, perception, judgment and action, restricting the flow of pure Intelligence. But as the more divine levels of Intelligence become awakened in the body, these negative qualities have a lesser influence, though they are still seen operating in individual and collective life.

The divine energy and intelligence of the subtle reality of the body is extremely powerful. It is this same flow of Cosmic Intelligence that creates and upholds the appearance of the universe. Some degree of this flow can initially be experienced as energy surges through the body. If the subtle channels in the body are blocked, these energy surges may not be very pleasant. In actuality, they are waves of divine bliss, but if the nervous system is not sufficiently refined, they can be experienced as pain and suffering. The nervous system needs to be cultured over time to be able to sustain these powerful bliss energies of divine Intelligence.

Clarity of refined perception results from past merit acquired due to subjecting the nervous system to powerful energy flows of transcendental bliss Consciousness through consistent systematic scientific spiritual practice.

All the qualities and functions of the mind and body are ultimately universal, cosmic and divine. Consciousness itself is not something that needs to be developed, refined or improved. It has always been whole and perfect. It only needs to be released from its false identification with the mind/body and objects of perception, and to open to the fullness of itself. When deep-rooted impressions and imbalances are gradually released and neutralized, the mind/body increasingly reflects the universal reality of the flow of Cosmic Intelligence out of which it is ultimately composed. Perception naturally opens to the subtle quantum field flows of cosmic life.

When the energy channels are clear, the flow of cosmic Intelligence is experienced as ever-increasing waves and flavors of boundless divine bliss. It may take many, many years of wave after wave of this bliss energy throughout the body before the perception of the subtle mechanics of creation begin to be clearly experienced. As this refinement continues, the finer qualities of cosmic Intelligence that create perception and experience are more clearly recognized and experienced on the surface of life. Life is the flow of cosmic Intelligence. It has always been divine, but now, perception refines to experience that reality.

Refined Perception in the state of Cosmic Consciousness has been referred to as "God Realization or God Consciousness". God Realization does not mean seeing or knowing God, or having faith or belief in God. It is human consciousness capable of experiencing and comprehending the subtle creative dynamics of God's creation. It is the perception of the subtle underlying Intelligence orchestrating life. It is Consciousness' experience of the finest relative aspect of itself.

The perception of this cosmic play of divine life continues to unfold in greater and greater clarity. Life is lived, not only from the field of unbounded pure Awareness, but also with clear perception of the subtle divine mechanics of creation that connect the unseen with the seen, and ultimately, create and control the appearance of everything. Like the brush strokes that create the image of a painting on the canvas, the flows of divine Cosmic Intelligence are creating the appearance of creation on the canvas of unbounded pure Awareness, your own true Self.

LIVING IN BLISS

As Consciousness deepens and perception refines, many profound changes take place in the body. The brain begins to function more holistically. New neural pathways are forged and unused areas begin to open and come alive. The brain is literally being rewired in order to connect to its true universal dimension and regain more of its cosmic utility. The brain is quantum mechanical and has always been cosmic, but it has been wired for mere individual physical experience due to the false identification with the mind and body.

Without this restoration, the true cosmic divine reality of life cannot be experienced. It can only be left to the concepts, beliefs, imaginations, fears or doubts of an unawakened mind. Refined Perception is the perception of this subtle reality of life. It is on the level of direct experience that cannot be known, even by the Awakened, without the necessary refinement of the finer levels of the brain and nervous system.

The body is made of the same qualities of intelligence that structure the universe. Its subtle reality is unbounded, cosmic and divine. The same cosmic Intelligence underlying, pervading and conducting the affairs of the universe, is responsible for the flow of thinking, feeling, perceiving, and all functions of the body. The body has always been a composite of frequencies of universal Intelligence. With sufficient refinement its subtle reality naturally opens to perception.

Cosmic Intelligence begins to awaken in the apparent individual body. The body can begin to experience spontaneous movements, postures, gestures and contortions as it adjusts to the awakening of these pure energy flows. Old stresses and impressions are thrown off, blockages are released, stuck emotions are cleared. Greater energy, lightness, smoothness, joy and bliss begin to flow through the body. Cosmic life awakens to itself through form.

Individual life begins to function more in tune with the universal flows of cosmic Intelligence. There is greater fluidity in the body, clarity in the senses, equanimity in mind, harmony in emotions, joyfulness in spirit, and lively bliss in the Being. Individual thought, feeling and action is supported by universal Intelligence. Greater access to the cosmic reservoir of strength, power, creativity and intelligence is available whenever the need arises.

Even on the physical level, the machinery of the body becomes more subtle and supple. The cosmic divine reality of the body awakens on the surface of life. Divine life walks, eats, talks, sees, hears, and acts through individual form. It sees itself in nature, in the surroundings, and in all life. It is the motivator of all actions and the mover of all things. It is the subtle cosmic energy and intelligence behind all knowing, feeling, doing, perceiving and experiencing.

The universal reality of individual appearance opens to perception and is lived in daily life. Every ordinary perception, thought, feeling and action is augmented by the cosmic divine Intelligence at the basis of life that is commanding and controlling it. There is no separate individual "me". There is just seeing, hearing, feeling, knowing, perceiving and doing, experienced in refined clarity as the flows of cosmic divine Intelligence.

Living in this state is living bliss. The waves of divine bliss can be so exquisite and intense at times that it may feel as though it cannot be contained. Yet, the mind and body continue to function normally and you appear quite ordinary to others. From this level, it is difficult to comprehend how problems, pain, suffering and mistakes have become the norm. The divine perfection of life is clearly experienced.

Throughout every perception, there is a superfluid flow of the frequencies of divine Intelligence orchestrating life. There is a great reverence, appreciation and surrender to the perfection and divine magnificence of it all. The mind, heart and soul are full with love, gratitude and surrender. Life is completely supported, nourished and protected in all circumstances. A deep compassion is felt for all human beings who still live in struggle and suffering, unaware of their true cosmic divine reality; yet, the perfection in that suffering is also seen. A natural desire arises to share this knowledge and experience to help others awaken to this reality. All thought and action are for the purpose of the upliftment and joy of life everywhere.

However, not everyone who awakens experiences the same degree of refined clarity and perception. On the level of Consciousness, we are all one, and we are all equal. But on the level of the refinement of the subtle levels of the nervous system, we are not. Everyone has been subjected to different intensities of physical, mental and emotional impressions and stresses over many years and lifetimes of false identification with the individual mind/body. This has constricted awareness, colored perception and limited experience in different ways in everyone.

Not only had we lost the experience of the unbounded universal reality of our true Self, but we have lost the experience of the universal divine reality of our personhood and perceptions. We have become limited to individuality. The body appears to be physical, but there is a subtler divine cosmic dimension to the body that the physical senses do not perceive. The world appears to be physical, but there is a subtler cosmic dimension to the world that the senses do not perceive.

Don't be fooled by the images your senses present to you. Don't be fooled by your thoughts and emotions. There is an aspect of your own mind, intellect, feelings, senses and entire body that is cosmic, unbounded, infinite and divine. You may not be in touch with it yet, but that does not mean that it does not exist. Not only does it exist, it is the ultimate source and reality of your existence.

Belief in God, or a higher power, is a beautiful thing, but directly experiencing and living the refined cosmic reality of your own mind/body, is on a completely different level. When experienced in its true cosmic status, your mind-body-personality *is* the universal personhood of Divine Cosmic Intelligence that is perpetually creating, guiding, upholding and recreating the appearance of the world and universe.

That infinite reality of divine Intelligence has been frozen in the appearance of individuality throughout many years and lifetimes of conditioning. It takes time to thaw. Infinite unbounded Pure Consciousness and the divine reality of life are here right now; but, it can take years in the enlightened state, and a good deal of holistic spiritual practice, to culture a deep, permanent level of true refined perception on the surface level of life. It is a gradual unfoldment that happens naturally, though slowly, being restricted to time and space. It can, however, be accelerated to some degree through holistic spiritual techniques practiced without effort or force.

REFINING PERCEPTION

There is no technique that can cause the shift to being Consciousness itself. The final stroke of Awakening happens beyond the mind and intellect to the innermost sense of being. Techniques can broaden awareness and help to balance and improve life, but they cannot cause the shift to Awakening. They are like the dawn that nourishes and awakens life, but the dawn cannot illumine the sun. Unbounded pure Awareness shines by itself on its own level.

The shift to being Awareness itself happens naturally of its own accord when the time is right, in spite of any technique, practice or belief. The idea of a "path" to enlightenment is one of the greatest barriers to Awakening. There is no path to the eternal present moment of Now. How can there be a path to what you already are? The real spiritual path begins *after* clear Awakening.

Many techniques are available for expanding consciousness and refining perception. However, not all techniques provide a balanced holistic growth and integrated unfoldment. Some techniques are useful for specific areas of the mind/body. Some are useful for certain levels of consciousness prior to awakening; and some are specific to higher States of Consciousness after Awakening. The knowledge of appropriate techniques for specific levels or states of Consciousness is a science, and should be transmitted by enlightened teachers with expertise in that area.

The intense practice of virtually any technique is bound to cause a spiritual experience of some sort. Spiritual experiences are wonderful, but spiritual experiences and true Awakening are two very different things. Spiritual experiences are temporary experiences that can happen as consciousness and perception are gradually unfolding. Real Awakening is the shift to being the source of all experience, and it is permanent. Spiritual experiences are not the goal of spiritual practice, nor are they a gauge of the level of evolution, or even the degree of readiness for Awakening.

The real value and purpose of spiritual practice is to systematically and scientifically culture and refine the mind, body and nervous system holistically, so that Consciousness can experience the maximum degree of clarity of perception from the broadest possible perspective.

The human body/mind is the expressed appearance of the total flow of Consciousness. It is the mechanism Consciousness uses to know the fullness of itself. The human being is the only species that comprises *all* the laws of nature that structure the appearance of the universe. This is why Consciousness can experience the maximum degree of itself through human appearance. The refinement of the subtle levels of the nervous system is necessary for this unfoldment.

The most beneficial techniques for balanced holistic unfoldment are those that effortlessly draw the attention beyond the mind, body and perceptions into the transcendental field of pure Awareness. Pure Awareness is a silent field of boundless peace, freedom and joy and the true nature of your inner Being. When the attention is naturally, effortlessly and spontaneously, drawn into deeper levels of inner silence and clear wakeful alertness, the body gains a profound state of deep physical rest. This enables the nervous system to heal and normalize so that it can maintain higher degrees of clarity of Consciousness.

The proper instruction, and regular practice of yoga asanas, pranayama and meditation techniques that produce deep rest and effortless transcending, are highly beneficial for anyone, regardless of what stage or state of Consciousness they may be experiencing.

All techniques of meditation that are natural, effortless and effective, originate from the natural process of transcending. Natural transcending is the experience of deep peace and equanimity. As Consciousness experiences itself even more deeply, intense waves of bliss energy can be experienced. This causes profound refinement to the body and mind. Yoga asanas, breathing practices and natural meditation techniques were originally cognized by seers who spontaneously experienced these bliss-energy flows and frequencies of cosmic Intelligence through their own bodies.

When the flow of cosmic Intelligence begins to be experienced on the physical level, the body naturally assumes positions or breathing patterns to accommodate that flow. In its effort to adjust and normalize, the body may go through all sorts of spontaneous movements. This is the natural process of the body refining to mirror the flow of nature's intelligence and returning to a more perfect style of functioning.

The body is the expressed appearance of the natural flow of divine Intelligence. It has lost its attunement with that natural flow of life due to conditioning which has resulted in physical, mental, emotional and spiritual impurities. This lack of attunement has created deep impressions in the mind, and stress in the nervous system. As these impurities get released and neutralized, the natural flow of energy and intelligence begins to return, and perception spontaneously refines to appreciate a more complete reality. Cosmic Intelligence continues to knead, mold and rarify the mind/body, until eventually the nervous system reflects more of its innate divine perfection.

Refined perception in the state of Cosmic Consciousness is the perception of the universal organizing Intelligence that underlies and orchestrates the physical appearance of life. But it is not seen from a complete perspective. The Self still remains the non-doing field of pure Awareness, the impartial Witness, in which all this is happening. There is still a distinction between silent, pure Being, and the alive flow of cosmic Intelligence responsible for the functioning of the body and world. Perception can be cultured to a great degree in this state, but Consciousness' perspective of itself is still incomplete because there is still a distinction between unbounded absolute pure Being and relative life.

It is only after the shift to Unity Consciousness that everything is experienced as being one wholeness. In this state, the same degree of Refined Perception is experienced from an entirely different perspective.

≈≈≈

CHAPTER TEN

CREATING THE APPEARANCE OF CREATION

Refined Perception in Unity Consciousness

FROM EXPERIENCING TO CREATING

The higher perspectives and perceptions of Consciousness that have been described are not philosophical ideas, or artificially altered states of consciousness. They are the direct experience of reality from the perspective of Consciousness itself, free from the false identification with the objects of experience, and seen through the unconditioned lens of a mind/body instrument functioning closer to the way it was originally designed.

In unawakened consciousness, "I" am the experiencer experiencing an experience, whatever it may be. In Cosmic Consciousness, "I" am the unbounded field of pure Awareness in which all experiencing and experience happens. In Unity Consciousness, "I" am the Oneness of experiencer, the process of experiencing and all experience. These are three distinctly different perspectives. As such, the very same degree of refinement of perception is experienced differently in each perspective.

In unawakened consciousness, it appears as if we are directly perceiving the world through our senses. But, we know from neuroscience, that our perception of the world "out there" is actually our mind's interpretation of the electrochemical signals in our brains. Everything we have ever experienced has been experienced within, and because of, consciousness.

To experience the existence of form and phenomena as we know it, there must be an experiencer and a process of experiencing. Without the senses and the processing mechanism of the brain, there is no such thing as objective physical phenomena. Without a perceiver to perceive it, and a mechanism to convert the electromagnetic energy in the environment into something meaningful, the so called "real physical world" would just be a mass of electromagnetic energy, as far as anyone knows.

Due to this, it is obvious that we have much more to do with the physical world around us than is immediately evident. The process of experiencing must have something to do with the process of creation. Whether or not we realize it, on an unconscious level, we are directly involved in the mechanics of creating the world around us.

Quantum physicists are very familiar with this phenomenon when trying to measure sub-atomic particles. They know that the act of measurement affects the outcome. This means that somehow *the conscious attention of the observer influences that which is being observed*. This is called the measurement problem in physics. It is a source of great puzzlement to physicists who do not yet realize the profundity of Consciousness and its relationship to our experience of the physical world.

Perception in Unity Consciousness is Consciousness' perception of its process of experiencing itself. Consciousness is not just awake to itself (as in Cosmic Consciousness); it is awake to its "process of being conscious of itself". In its process of being conscious of itself, Consciousness flows in waves of pure Intelligence. Perception refines to experience these flows of Intelligence within Consciousness.

These flows of universal Intelligence give rise to all experience. They are everywhere, underlying, permeating, pervading and creating the appearance of everything. Cosmic Intelligence has been governing every aspect of life all along whether we have been aware of it or not. The ordinary action of perceiving and experiencing, which appears to be happening through the individual brain and senses, is now seen to be the action of the flow of the field of Consciousness awake within itself. This action of Consciousness, which is the flow of universal Intelligence, gives rise to the *appearance* of the objects and phenomena of perception and experience.

From this refined perspective, *it is directly experienced that you, as Consciousness, are creating the appearance of the world around you, including your own body.* Consciousness is not only the experiencer, the process of experiencing and all experience—it is the creator, the process of creating, and all creation.

The flows of Intelligence within Consciousness are creating the appearance of all form and phenomena of experience. The world is the expressed appearance of these streams of universal Intelligence inherent in Consciousness. Deep within the unconscious cosmic aspect of your own mind, universal Intelligence is creating and recreating the appearance of the world around you every split-second, right now.

These flows of universal Intelligence are the same quantum fields that physicists are investigating. Only, they are intimately experienced as the alive flows of your own SELF from the total perspective of Unity Consciousness, rather than as elementary particles of matter in a universe separate from you, from the incomplete perspective of unawakened consciousness. When clearly perceived, this quantum field flow of life is a far more substantial reality than the physical world and universe. From this holistic perspective, the paradoxes, mysteries and limitations of today's science are easily seen through.

QUANTUM FIELD PERCEPTION

Quantum Mechanics is the investigation into the physical behavior of molecules, atoms and subatomic particles. These atomic and subatomic levels function according to a radically different set of rules from the physics of the visible universe. Particles are unpredictable and unlocalized. They can act like waves; they can be in more than one place at the same time. They can tunnel through walls, be entangled even though separated by great distances, and be affected by the knowledge of an observer. Scientists are perplexed by the strange behavior of the quantum mechanical world.

These elementary particles are the building blocks of the universe. But in reality, they are not even real physical particles. They are high density vortex-like points of unbounded quantum probability fields of all possibility that could extend to infinity, as far as anyone knows. Most physicists have concluded that the fundamental reality of the universe is actually unbounded quantum fields, not particles.

What we think of as particles are actually points of excitation of those unbounded quantum fields and the epiphenomena that arises from them. Just the fact that all physical matter (including your own body) is made up of elementary particles that are not at all physical, have no distinct boundaries, and are excitations of unbounded fields of infinite potentiality, clearly demonstrates the true unseen unbounded reality of life.

These unbounded fields are actually frequencies of the flow of Consciousness. They are qualities of the flow of Intelligence generated within Consciousness in its experience of itself. Each apparent particle is a point value excitation of an unbounded frequency (or set of frequencies) of the flow of infinite Consciousness.

Ever in its process of being conscious of itself, Consciousness is an unlimited field of infinite potentiality. It is the universal quantum field of all possibilities. It is your own unbounded Being, freed from the false identification with individual mind and open to the total flow of the fullness of itself. The unbounded matter and energy fields that give rise to the appearance of the universe are the reverberating fluctuations of pure energy and intelligence of the flow of Consciousness in the activity of being conscious of itself.

These fluctuations are not just out there somewhere at subtler levels of energy and matter. They are the universal reality of your own mind, body, senses, personality and fine feelings. They are the finer levels of your own total Being. Consciousness conscious of itself is the quantum field mechanics that gives rise to the appearance of the universe. Everything that appears to be physical is the concretized appearance of the unseen flows of universal Intelligence of the unbounded reality of your own Consciousness.

From the perspective of Unity Consciousness, quantum mechanics is not at all mysterious. It is simple. The world out here is not an actual objective physical reality. It is the subjective experience of the *appearance* of an objective physical world, created by the quantum field flows of universal Intelligence at the subtlest level of our mind and brain. It is the display of the internal dynamics of Consciousness. Physicists are unknowingly researching into the finer levels of the universal reality of their own mind, body, feelings and personality.

However, the mind is an object of experience, and as such, it is incapable of investigating into the true reality of the internal dynamics of Consciousness. You have to *be* Consciousness to experience and comprehend its flow. This is why quantum mechanics remains such a mystery to scientists. It is in the realm of Consciousness and can only be comprehended by Consciousness, not by the individual mind.

Refined perception in Unity Consciousness begins when the SELF clearly experiences these frequencies of the flow of Consciousness on the surface appearance of life. It is as though the unbounded SELF sees itself looking back at itself from every point within itself. Seeing itself at a point within itself is a motion in one direction; recognizing its infinity at that point is a motion in the other direction. Each recognition of the pure clarity of the infinite reality of itself is a wave of bliss in the ocean of Being and reverberates throughout creation.

Consciousness is perpetually flowing from its infinity to a point within itself to know itself, and instantaneously expanding in tidal waves of bliss in the recognition of its own boundless infinity at that point. This is what is creating the vibrant, alive wakefulness within the unbounded silence of pure Awareness. It is creating the incentive for universal Intelligence to flow in the appearance of creation. It is creating the pure Alertness that enables all your thoughts, sensations and perceptions of the world around you to be experienced right now.

It is this internal dynamic within Consciousness that is causing the alive Presence in the space around you. Presence is the product of the Aliveness of the unbounded fullness of your total Being. It is the flow of your own SELF awake within itself.

BEING ALIVENESS

Consciousness is Consciousness because it is conscious of itself at every point within itself. It is a non-moving, non-doing, infinite, silent field of pure Awareness moving and doing in its process of experiencing itself. It is infinite Silence in flow, ever awake to itself everywhere within itself.

It is the Aliveness of the Presence in the space around you right now. It is the subtle energy within every object in your range of perception and beyond. It is the silent knowing of the awakened intellect, the quiet alertness of the mind, the pure clarity of the senses, the subtle energetic liveliness in your body.

Everything is alive with Intelligence. This is the nature of pure Consciousness itself. It is the SELF in its process of experiencing itself.

Allow your attention to be with the Presence around you...

It's an Alive Presence

A sense that something is watching you

It is a watching Presence

A watching Awareness

Watching from everywhere

It is watching you now

Innocently be with that watching Presence...

As the sense of Watching Presence increases,

Stillness increases

As the Stillness increases,

Aliveness increases...

Awareness becomes more awake,

more alert

more present in the moment

163

there is more expansion

more spaciousness

Attention is more focused

perception is clearer

The Aliveness in the Presence around you is palpable...

That Alive Presence is not foreign. It is familiar. There is nothing to fear.

It is your mind experiencing the subtle activity within the boundlessness of your own Consciousness.

The wakeful, alert Awareness of your own boundless Being *is* the Aliveness of the silent Presence all around you.

Experienced on its own level in the state of Unity Consciousness, that Alive Presence is pure Consciousness perpetually experiencing itself at every point within itself in the process of being awake to its own infinity. It is the boundless expanse of your own SELF in its process of knowing itself.

When experienced on its own level, beyond the experiencer and all experience, that Aliveness is pure Intelligence. Even though you may not be aware of it, you are beginning to open to the fundamental universal frequencies of energy and Intelligence within the unbounded reality of your total Being. These frequencies are responsible for creating the appearance of the world around you.

This may be just a vague sense or a concept for you at this time. But, after Awakening to Unity Consciousness, if perception is sufficiently refined, you will experience firsthand that the aliveness in the Presence around you is your own SELF in its activity of knowing itself, and that it is a boundless universal field of pure Intelligence. It is the cosmic aspect of your own mind, the quantum field reality of your brain and body, and the ultimate source and flow of all your perceptions of the world and universe.

The alive flow of Consciousness (experienced in its fullness in refined Unity Consciousness) is the universal Intelligence creating the appearance of all perceptions. It is the universal reality of your own mind and body. It is your SELF.

The only reason this has not been your direct experience is because the habitual experience of physical appearance has been overshadowing the true unbounded quantum field reality of your total Being. The clear experience of *being* the boundless wholeness of Consciousness and its fine frequencies and flows of Intelligence that appear as all form and phenomena, is what is meant by Refined Perception in Unity Consciousness.

THE FLOW OF INTELLIGENCE

Consciousness conscious of itself is the flow of pure Intelligence. Pure Intelligence is inherent in pure Consciousness. The maintenance of the integrity of all form and phenomena within the dynamics of perpetual change is the display of this Intelligence. Change itself is the flow of universal Intelligence. There are infinite levels and degrees of intensity of flow of Intelligence inherent in the infinity of Consciousness. Universal Intelligence is creating, maintaining and appearing as life on all levels of creation simultaneously.

It is the boundless field of infinite potentiality, the whirling atoms and particles of the quantum world, and the form and phenomena of the physical world and universe. It functions as your cells, your organs, your entire body, mind and heart. It governs all of nature, upholds the motion of the planets and orchestrates the entire cosmos. It is everywhere creating, maintaining and appearing as everything on all levels of life. It is the flow of the wholeness of Life.

You may think the space, air, light and the objects around you are not conscious Intelligence, and have nothing to do with you, but that is only because you are not yet conscious of the total reality of your existence. When you are fully Awakened, everything is Consciousness, everything is Intelligence, everything is "my SELF".

There are many levels of the flow of infinite Intelligence, and many degrees of clarity and intensity within each level. It is experienced in different ways by different people depending upon the refinement of the nervous system. All spiritual experiences are a taste of some degree of this flow of pure Divine energy and Intelligence.

When the flow of Intelligence is not experienced in its unconditioned pure flow, the mind can create ideas, images, objects and phenomena that may appear to be out there somewhere separate from you. But there is nothing separate from you on the level of Consciousness. Everything is the flow of your SELF within itself. Entertaining ideas of extraterrestrial or celestial beings based on a partial understanding or experience can create concepts, beliefs and imaginations that may cause you to chase after (or fear) something that is unreal. Or it may inflate the ego if you take importance from your experience. Both can be a barrier to clear Awakening.

When the flow of Consciousness is experienced in its clarity, without the interference of the individual mind, it is the simple pure flow of the universal divine Intelligence of the SELF in its process of experiencing the fullness of itself—and it is exquisite.

All existence is the expression of the flow of the infinite Intelligence inherent in Consciousness. Your individual mind/ body is the appearance of a concentrated point of the infinite wholeness of pure Intelligence, and the universe is the expressed appearance of its infinity. The activity of reading, perceiving and experiencing the world around you, taking place right now, is the flow of universal Intelligence. It is the activity of the subtle functioning of the unlocalized reality of the cosmic aspect of your own mind.

Universal Intelligence is constantly flowing to your senses in the form of the electromagnetic energy in the environment around you. The subtle quantum field reality of your brain is continuously creating the images of the world out of that flow of Consciousness. Your body and the world around you are the physical expressions of the subtle flow of universal pure Consciousness. Flowing to a point within itself to experience its own infinity, universal Consciousness appears as individual consciousness. The individual mind/body appearance is the means for Consciousness to experience the details of the infinity of itself in the appearance of the world and universe. This subtle action of perceiving and experiencing that you experience every waking moment, is the individualized experience of the flow of the universal Intelligence of Consciousness being conscious of itself.

This flow of Intelligence is happening at every point everywhere. Everything you see, including your own body, is the display of the flow of infinite creative intelligence. It is the play of infinite Consciousness awake to itself at every point within itself. It is the experiencer, the process of experiencing and the experience. It is perpetually referring back to itself at every point in its process of being conscious of itself and instantaneously expanding to its infinity. It is this lively impulse of pure Intelligence, inherent everywhere in the nature of infinite Consciousness, that generates the flow of creative intelligence that creates the appearance of the form and phenomena of experience, including that of your own mind and body.

You *are* that flow. You *are* the appearance. Everything is SELF.

This action of Consciousness, conscious of itself, gives rise to countless oscillations and waves of Intelligence in the ocean of Being. Like an interference pattern created when two waves collide, Infinite Consciousness flows in multiple waves of creative intelligence. These waves of the flow of infinity are not chaotic. Consciousness, in its pure state, is a field of perfect Silence, and as such, it is perfect order. Being absolute pure order, it flows in perfect rhythmic waves and frequencies of divine organizing power and intelligence. It is the lively, energetic excitation at the finest universal level of your total Being.

These frequencies of the flow of divine Intelligence are reverberations of your own unbounded Consciousness. They are the infallible cosmic laws that uphold the vast expanse of the appearance of the universe. All levels of the appearance of life are created and sustained by these flows of universal Intelligence. Each frequency of the flow, being a wave of divine energy and Intelligence, has a specific structure, quality and function. They each have an individual existence, and yet each wave is the flow of one Life. They are individual waves, yet they are the flow of the wholeness of boundless pure Consciousness.

These reverberant vibrations of Consciousness are not frequencies of inert matter or lifeless energy. They are waves of supremely divine Intelligence and bliss. A clear experience of even a tiny ripple of one of these pure frequencies within the boundlessness of your Being, is extraordinarily rapturous and sublime.

Some degree of that Intelligence can be felt by anyone at any time by just being still and innocently being awake to the Presence in the room around you.

When you are still, you can feel an alive Presence underlying and pervading everything within and all around you...

That Presence you feel is not actually in the room; the room, your body, and all your perceptions are in that Presence. Presence is not actually an experience; it is the effect produced by the unbounded reality of the Awareness that is aware of it. It is your own Consciousness. It is the presence of your own unbounded pure Awareness.

Within that Presence is the subtle sense of alive, watching Awareness: a liveliness in the Presence around you watching your eyes read these words. It can be felt in the entire field of your vision right now...

It is everywhere...

    above your head

    behind you

    in the space between your eyes and this page

It is all around you...

    it underlies and pervades everything

    it permeates your body

    it is everywhere, permeating everything

It is everything...

In refined Unity Consciousness, that alive Presence of your own SELF in its perpetual experience of itself, is creating and appearing as the world around you. The hidden process of the flow of pure experiencing becomes the dominant experience. The process of experiencing *is* the process of creating. It is the flow of Intelligence inherent in the nature of silent, pure Awareness.

That Aliveness you are sensing is not actually *in* anything; everything *is* that Aliveness in appearance. All the objects and phenomena you are experiencing right now, including your own body, are the expressed appearance of that Aliveness. They are that Aliveness shaped into the appearance of form by the quantum field creative intelligence of the cosmic aspect of your own mind.

It is the flow of your own SELF within itself. It is the same sense of Being you have been all along, only experiencing itself in its fullness as the flow of Intelligence creating and appearing as all form and phenomena. All phenomenal experience, no matter how real or unreal, whether physical, spiritual or divine, is the expressed appearance of that infinitely dynamic self-interacting unbounded field of pure Consciousness awake within itself.

On its own level, that vibrant field of boundless Consciousness is an unbounded ocean of infinite potentiality—a limitless, teeming caldron of infinite Intelligence, reverberating with all possibilities. The individual life you are experiencing now is only one such possibility. But, at a deeper level within and beyond that individual life, you *are* that alive flow of infinite possibility. You are unbounded pure Consciousness fully awake in its refined experience of itself appearing as everything everywhere.

THE UNCREATED UNIVERSE

Time and space, though appearing to be in the physical world, are actually inherent in Consciousness. The timeless flow of unbounded Consciousness in its perpetual process of knowing itself, appears as the passage of time and distance in space when perceived from the perspective of the conditioned individual mind. This is why time and space still remain a great mystery to scientists. But the distance in space is simply the mind's perception from one point to another point in the boundlessness of pure Awareness. The passage of time is the mind's perception of the flow of timeless pure Consciousness in its process of being conscious of itself.

The flow of Consciousness creates the appearance of all variations of energy and form. It is the true source of all time, space, energy and matter. It is the substance of all matter. Matter is energy in appearance. Energy is the flow of intelligence. Intelligence is the flow of Consciousness. All forms of matter and energy are different intensities and densities of the perpetual flow of the universal field of Consciousness. The underlying essence and fundamental basis of everything we see as the manifest world, including all variations of space, time, energy, heat, light, liquidity and solidity, are naturally inherent in the structure of unmanifest pure Consciousness.

It appears as though it has taken billions of years for the universe to form and somehow create the condition for life to begin, eventually creating a habitat suitable for mankind. But this is only true from the perspective of the mind caught in time and space and identified with the objects of experience. When Awareness is freed from the false identification with the mind and has the refined perception capable of perceiving its own internal dynamics, it is Self-evident that the universe is being created and recreated instantaneously and continuously in Consciousness by Consciousness in the timeless eternal moment of Now.

Your real SELF is timeless pure Consciousness moving within itself in its process of being conscious of itself, creating the sense of time and space and all the fundamental levels of energy and intelligence responsible for the appearance of the world and universe. The world around you right now is being created and sustained in the timeless field of unbounded pure Consciousness by the universal Intelligence of the cosmic aspect of your own mind.

≈≈≈

CHAPTER ELEVEN

BEHIND THE APPEARANCE

PHYSICS AND CONSCIOUSNESS

This chapter is bound to take you into the mind. So, if you have not yet awakened, or are not intellectually oriented, just read this easily without the need for understanding. However, if you would like to gain a deeper insight as to how Consciousness and the universe are related (which may challenge your concepts about your perceptions of the world) you may get some joy out of this, especially if you have already awakened. In any case, be innocently awake to the alive Presence everywhere in the room around you, and allow the mind and intellect to do whatever they have to do.

The Aliveness you sense in the Presence around you, when experienced in its pure flow, is Consciousness falling back upon itself to know itself, and simultaneously, instantaneously expanding at every point within itself in the remembrance of its infinity. It is reverberating pure universal Intelligence. It is the subtle universal aspect of your own mind and the quantum field reality of your own brain. The objects and phenomena experienced by your senses are the expressed appearance of that reverberating Pure Intelligence shaped into form through creative intention, memory and repetitive experience. Your individual mind/body is the expressed appearance of the total dynamics of that flow of universal Intelligence of Consciousness experiencing itself at a point.

We have become so obsessed with the appearance created by the flow of Consciousness that we have been completely lost to the deeper reality of our SELF and its mechanics of knowing. This accounts for the great discrepancy between the physics of the observable universe which describes the obvious, and the mathematics of quantum physics, which expresses a deeper reality of our Being.

From the perspective of refined Unity Consciousness, the quantum field realm is directly experienced as being the flow of the SELF in its perpetual experience of itself, creating the *appearance* of particles and form. All creation, from the microscopic levels of quantum mechanics to the macrocosmic levels of the universe, is the expressed appearance of the innumerable frequencies of the flow of universal Intelligence generated by Consciousness in its process of being conscious of itself.

The mysterious phenomena in quantum mechanics known as the *collapse of the wave function* (the transition from the super-position of all possible states to a single discrete state due to the act of observation), is not at all mysterious from the perspective of refined Unity Consciousness. This collapse is naturally inherent in Consciousness in its action of being conscious of itself and is part of the subtle mechanics of creation that gives rise to the perception of form and phenomena.

The *cosmological inflation theory* (the rapid exponential expansion of the universe seconds after the Big Bang) provides a glimpse into what happens on a cosmic scale when Consciousness awakens to its infinity. As Consciousness collapses to a point within itself to know itself, it instantly expands in the remembrance of its infinity at that point. Consciousness is perpetually collapsing to a point within itself to know itself and instantaneously expanding to its infinite reality at that point. This dynamic interaction between these two apparently opposing forces sets into motion the quantum field flows of energy and intelligence responsible for creating the appearance of particles, form and phenomena.

The seemingly unrelated phenomena of the "collapse of the wave function" and "cosmological inflation", when stripped free from the notions of time, space, particles and form, are actually expressions of the one continuous flow of Consciousness in its perpetual process of being conscious of itself. All levels of creation are the expressed appearance of the dynamic flows of energy and intelligence inherent in the action of Consciousness being conscious of itself.

The mysterious forces of "dark matter" and "dark energy" are also examples of the effect of this flow of Consciousness. *Dark matter* is a hypothetical invisible matter comprising over 80% of the total mass of the universe. It is thought to be the force responsible for holding the elements of the universe together. *Dark energy* is the name given to an unseen force thought to be responsible for accelerating the expansion of the universe. Physicists know these forces exist due to the effect they have on matter and the large-scale structure of the universe, but they have no idea what they really are.

These forces are not at all mysterious or dark from the perspective of Consciousness. They are the effect produced by the total flow of Consciousness in its perpetual experience of itself. "Dark Matter" is the effect of the force of Consciousness collapsing back upon itself to experience itself. It is the binding force of universal Intelligence that holds Consciousness in the appearance of form. This is the same force as the act of observation causing the "collapse of the wave function", as mentioned previously. This force is the fundamental cause of the Strong Force that binds together protons in the nucleus of the atom on the quantum level, and it is the underlying basis of the force of gravity on the physical level of life.

"Dark Energy" is actually the effect of the exponential expansion perpetually happening everywhere within Consciousness in its process of awakening to its infinity. From the perspective of the mind caught in time and space, it appears as though an unknown force of dark energy is accelerating the expansion of the universe. But from the perspective of refined Unity Consciousness, it is seen that it is not that the universe is accelerating in its expansion; it is that Consciousness itself is naturally expanding at every point within itself in its perpetual remembrance of its infinity. It is the same force causing the hypothetical phenomena of "cosmological inflation".

The real reason dark energy and dark matter have never been directly perceived is because they are not phenomena of the "physical" universe; they are properties of the consciousness of the scientist. These forces are naturally inherent in Consciousness in its process of being conscious of itself. They are two aspects of the same one flow of Consciousness.

It is amazing that scientists can conceptualize and calculate what possibly happened in the first seconds after the Big Bang, or what is happening in the outer vastness of infinite space or in the microscopic world of quantum physics. But, where did those observations, insights and calculations actually happen? In the consciousness of the scientist, of course. Knowledge is inherent in the structure of Consciousness. Consciousness is the fundamental source of everything.

The physical senses perceive form and phenomena, but they do not perceive the flow of Intelligence that is creating the appearance of form. All the fundamental forces of nature are the effect of the flow of Consciousness. Consciousness is the ultimate *Unified Field* (the attempt to describe all fundamental forces and the relationships between elementary particles in a single theoretical framework in physics).

The total flow of boundless pure Consciousness in its perpetual process of experiencing itself gives rise to the endless play and display of the appearance of the universe. The created appearance is sustained and maintained by the universal flow of pure memory within in the cosmic aspect of individual and collective mind.

When seen as it actually is, the universe is a projection of the frequencies of the eternal memory inherent in Consciousness. Consciousness is Consciousness because it is ever in the process of knowing and remembering itself. It is a field of pure Memory, a field of pure Knowledge. The reverberations of the flow of Consciousness are the frequencies of pure Memory. They are not memories or knowledge of specific events or occurrences, but the eternal Memory of the reverberant frequencies of the flow of pure Intelligence inherent in Consciousness.

The quantum field flows of energy and intelligence, in the quantum world of physics and mathematics, are actually frequencies of the flow of the eternal Memory of Consciousness of itself. The flow of universal Intelligence is the eternal Memory Bank of pure Consciousness in motion. It is pure Memory.

Every physical, mental, emotional and spiritual phenomena and form is the appearance generated by the flows of the infinite energy and Intelligence of Consciousness knowing itself. They are the expressed appearance of the pure Memory inherent in Consciousness. The universe is the image of the pure Memory. It is not the result of some happenstance cosmic event in time and space that happened billions of years ago. Creation is the display of the frequencies of eternal Memory. This is the underlying premise behind the theory of the "Akashic records" (the compilation of all human events, thoughts, words, emotions, and intent ever to have occurred in the past, present, or future).

This is also akin to what physicists have proposed in the Holographic Theory of the universe. This theory claims that the universe is a three-dimensional projection of the information contained in a two-dimensional field. It could also be said that the universe is a three-dimensional projection from the perspective of Unity Consciousness. But the two-dimensional field is the infinitely horizontal and infinitely vertical dimensionless field of the flow of unbounded pure Consciousness in its eternal process of being conscious of itself.

As a dream is a thought created by your own mind out of your own consciousness, the universe is a thought created by the cosmic aspect of your mind, from the unmanifest field of the pure Memory and Intelligence inherent in infinite pure Consciousness in its perpetual process of being conscious of itself.

YOU ARE THE CREATOR

Everyone has a similar experience of the world because, at the most fundamental level of our Being, we are all the same one Consciousness. Consciousness is an unbounded field of pure Intelligence, vibrant and alive with infinite potentiality and all possibility. This infinite Intelligence in Consciousness is the universal aspect of your own mind. It is this universal Intelligence that is creating the appearance of the objects and phenomena around you, including that of your own body. Your conditioned individual mind creates its own little world view and life situation out of that unbounded field of infinite potentiality.

As we know from neuroscience, the world "out there" is actually our mind's interpretation of the electrical and electromagnetic processes in our brain. But what is missing in this understanding is that the electromagnetic field and the fundamental forces of the universe are also not a physical reality. They are the non-local unbounded flows of Intelligence in the field of pure Awareness of the consciousness of the observer. They are the flows of intelligence of the quantum field reality of your brain. Electromagnetic energy is actually an expressed level of unlocalized field reverberations of the flow of Consciousness in its process of experiencing itself. All the fundamental forces of nature are levels of the flow of Intelligence in your own unbounded Awareness. They are reverberations of Consciousness.

Consciousness is not contained in the individual mind or brain because our mind, brain and body are not individual—they are cosmic. The quantum field reality of the brain is the cosmic aspect of your own mind. So, the process of perceiving is not just happening in your individual mind or brain. It is happening at every point in the entire field of your perception and experience. Perception only appears to be taking place from the individual to the objects in the surroundings. But in actuality, the universal Intelligence of the cosmic aspect of your own mind is creating your perceptions of the world around you every split second at every point in your surroundings simultaneously, out of the fabric of the boundless field of your own Awareness.

The process of perceiving the world around you is actually the *process of creating* that is taking place in the cosmic aspect of your mind. When you think you are experiencing something, you are actually creating your own experience. The pure Intelligence of the quantum field reality of your brain and universal Intelligence of your own mind, is creating, maintaining and recreating the solid physical appearance of your body and the world around you right now.

Your brain appears to be individual, but it is quantum mechanical and cosmic. It is the individualized appearance of the quantum field dynamics of infinite Consciousness. You have a cosmic mind, a cosmic brain, a cosmic Consciousness, whether you are aware of it or not. The world only appears to be a physical reality out there somewhere separate from you from the perspective of an individual mind identified with the objects of its experience. The universe is inherent in the structure of Consciousness in a perpetual state of infinite potentiality. It has never come into existence as a separate solid reality on its own. It is only an appearance generated by the continuous perpetual activity of Consciousness conscious of itself.

This is the direct experience from the perspective of refined Unity Consciousness. In this state, it is an obvious reality that the flow of Intelligence inherent in Consciousness is the creator, the process of creating and the creation. The quantum field intelligence of the cosmic reality of your brain (the flow of Consciousness) is continually creating the appearance of your body and the world around you. You are creating your own individual experience out of the universal sea of infinite potentiality of unbounded pure Consciousness. Your experience of the world is uniquely individual, yet distinctly universal.

From the perspective of Consciousness itself, it could also be said that there is no creation. It is all just Consciousness being conscious of itself. It is eternal, and it is uncreated. Creation is only an appearance, not a reality. This goes beyond understanding to become the direct experience in the state beyond SELF (described in Part IV). Like the unpainted image in the mind of a painter, the physical universe is only an idea in the universal mind of unmanifest pure Consciousness.

The experience of reality depends upon the perspective from which it is viewed. When you view yourself and the world from the perspective of individual mind identified with the objects of experience, it will only provide a limited, partial viewpoint. But you are not the mind, you are the Awareness that is aware of it. When viewed from the perspective of unbounded Awareness in the state of Cosmic Consciousness, it is also an incomplete perspective. Consciousness, in that state, is not fully awake to the total reality of itself. Even in the state of Unity Consciousness, Consciousness may not yet be clearly awake to its process of experiencing itself.

In refined Unity Consciousness, Consciousness is fully awake to itself as being everything everywhere and clearly awake to its process of experiencing itself. In this state, the divine energy and Intelligence of the flow of Consciousness, which is creating the appearance of creation, can begin to be appreciated in greater fullness.

We have been caught in the surface appearance of the world of form and phenomena, which can be beautiful on its own level. But seeing it in its total reality by *being* the clarity and purity of the flow of Consciousness that is essentially creating and appearing as it all, is far more profound, exquisitely beautiful and divine.

COSMIC PERSON-CENTERED UNIVERSE

Your body appears to be individual and separate, but, on a deeper level, beyond the range of your senses, your body is quantum mechanical and universal. The quantum level of the brain and body is the same for everyone and it is the underlying reality of the universe. From the perspective of refined Unity Consciousness, the quantum field level is found to be an aspect of your own SELF. It is ultimately, the flow of Consciousness in its process of being conscious of itself. It is a field of infinite potentiality and all possibility. All the qualities of Intelligence and laws of nature that structure the appearance of the universe are inherent within it.

Your individual mind/body is the expressed appearance of that total flow of Consciousness *at a point*. All the qualities of Intelligence and laws of nature are present at the point of your apparent individual mind/body. At the subtle quantum field level, your body and the universe are the same one field of infinite potentiality. When Awareness is awake to that level, the world and universe are found to be the expressed appearance of the subtle quantum field reality of your own body. *At the quantum field level, you are the universe.* To get a clearer sense of why this is so, it is important to get a better feel for the internal dynamics of Consciousness.

Consciousness is Consciousness because it is conscious of itself everywhere within itself. This means that the Awareness through which you are experiencing right now is Awareness, not because *you have awareness*, but because *you are Awareness*; and Awareness is naturally aware of itself everywhere within the boundlessness of itself.

It is your real Self—who you really are.

It only appears as if you are an individual person separate from your surroundings because you have become overly identified with the individual body/mind and its perceptions and are still conditioned to that experience.

Pure Awareness, aware of itself, is the universal sense of Being and Existing. It is the same sense of being and existing you are experiencing right now, only not limited to your mind and body. It is the unbounded, universal, absolute, non-changing, non-moving, non-doing pure Being.

Its boundless reality can be felt to some extent right now as the silent Presence and Stillness in the room around you...

Pure Awareness, awake to its process of being conscious of itself, is the act of Knowing. Knowing is inherent in Being. Knowing is infinitely dynamic and alive. It is Consciousness in the dynamic flow of knowing itself. This action of Knowing, everywhere in the infinity of Consciousness, is universal Intelligence. Universal Intelligence creates, orchestrates and creates the appearance of all life on all levels of creation. It is the universal aspect of your mind, intellect, feelings, senses and entire personhood.

That universal field of Intelligence can be sensed, to some degree, as the Aliveness of the watching Presence in the space around you right now...

That Aliveness is your own unbounded Awareness in its action of knowing itself. In its perpetual process of knowing itself, Consciousness is continuously collapsing back upon itself at every point and instantaneously expanding in the recognition of its own infinity. This perpetual motion in Consciousness creates the light of Awareness that illumines all cognition and perception, enabling you to comprehend, perceive and experience right here and now.

This constant reverberation of Consciousness creates innumerable waves, frequencies and qualities of Intelligence within itself, while remaining one unmodified unbounded silent ocean of pure Consciousness. These reverberations are the primal flows of universal energy and Intelligence that structure the appearance of form. Your entire person is made of the material of universal Intelligence. The laws that govern the formation and function of every aspect of your mind and body are universal.

There is no aspect of yourself that is individual or personal. Universal Intelligence causes your mind to think, your feelings to feel, your senses to perceive, your heart to beat, and all other functions of your mind and body. Universal Intelligence has been governing your life all along.

Universal Intelligence not only governs your life, it *is* your life. All the qualities and functions of your entire person are frequencies of the quantum field flows of universal Intelligence. The subtle reality of your personhood, free from all stresses, past impressions and karmas incurred due to false identification with the individual mind/body appearance, is a Universal Personality.

The Aliveness in the Presence around you, experienced in its refined clarity in fully awakened Consciousness, is that universal Personality. It is the subtle universal aspect of your own mind/body, the quantum field level of life, and the underlying substance of all life. *The quantum field level of life is the universal aspect of your own personhood.* It is the subtle cosmic reality of your total Being. Your entire person is inherent in the eternal flow of Consciousness in the process of experiencing itself. The universal aspect of your personhood is the inherent structure of Consciousness itself.

As an elementary particle is a high density point of an unbounded particle field, the human being is a high density point of the total energy and Intelligence of infinite Consciousness. As a whirlpool is a vortex in the ocean, your personhood is a vortex of the total potential of the energy and Intelligence in the unbounded ocean of Consciousness.

Your true SELF, which has been seemingly limited to your mind and body, is actually everything everywhere in your field of awareness right now, and has been so all along. It is unbounded, infinite, timeless and eternal, and your total person is everywhere within its flow. The perception of the changing world around you is the appearance created by that flow of Consciousness in the process of knowing itself. It is the expressed appearance of the universal reality of your own personality. It is Consciousness in appearance.

Consciousness is the experiencer, the process of experiencing and all experience—the oneness of *Knower, Knowing and Known.* Just as the quantum vacuum level, the quantum mechanical level, and the physical level of life are distinct levels of the universe governed by specific laws, the *Knower,* the process of *Knowing* and the *Known* are distinct modes within the oneness of Consciousness. Each mode has its own set of reverberant frequencies of Intelligence. Each set of frequencies is an elaboration of the previous.

The information within the silent *Knower* of pure Being becomes lively Intelligence through the activity of Consciousness *Knowing* itself, which creates the appearance of the *Known* universe. The *Known* universe is the expressed appearance of the universal Intelligence of *the process of Knowing,* which is the excitation of the latent information inherent in the *Knower.* It is all one flow of Consciousness in its perpetual process of knowing itself. It is an alive field of infinite Intelligence and all possibility.

Your entire person is cosmic. It is structured in the very nature of Consciousness conscious of itself and it appears as everything in your field of perception. All your perceptions of the world are the expressed appearance of the universal frequencies of the cosmic reality of your personhood. The universe, and everything in it, is the manifest appearance of the multifarious configurations of the structure, qualities and functions of your own personhood, created by the universal Intelligence of the cosmic quantum field reality of your own brain.

Everything you have ever experienced in the world is the manifest appearance of some aspect of the cosmic reality of your own person. When an astronomer looks through a telescope at the universe "out there", he is actually looking at a snapshot of the cosmic aspect of his own brain. The universe is the cosmic extension of your mind and body. It is all Consciousness. It is all your SELF.

Take a little break from your mind for a minute.

Innocently be with the Stillness in the space around you...

There is no need to understand or to learn this.

Just innocently notice your eyes seeing
Notice your mind reading the words

If some understanding happens: that's good.
If no understanding happens: that's even better.

UNIVERSAL YOU

The formless frequencies and flavors of the flow of Intelligence that appear as all creation are the one universal Personality of Infinite Consciousness. It is your own personality experienced from the perspective of fully awakened Consciousness.

Your individual body/personality only appears to be physical due to the incomplete experience of the total reality of your SELF.

When the SELF experiences the fine flavors of the flow of Intelligence within itself, the universal reality of the individual personality is revealed. All aspects of the apparent individual personality are perceived, as they really are, in their cosmic unbounded status. Your own body/mind/personality, when experienced with refined clarity, is revealed to be universal and divine. The human being is an infinite Being at its core, and a Divine Being in its constitution.

The more clearly Consciousness experiences the finer flows of its own pure Light, the more the body and its perceptions are bathed in that flow of light. The brain and nervous system function at a more refined level and the perception of the finer quantum field flows of Intelligence that appear as all life is experienced at all times. Though perfection may not be found on the physical level of life, the divine perfection underlying and pervading the appearance of life is experienced right on the surface. All objects and phenomena are the appearance created by the flows of the divine perfection of your own Consciousness. It is only necessary to refine perception to experience the divine perfection that has been there all along.

The laws that govern the functioning of the body, world and universe are mathematically precise because they are the eternal flows of universal Intelligence inherent in Consciousness. The creative Intelligence of the universal aspect of mind creates the images, forms and phenomena found in nature and the universe out of the formless flows of divine Intelligence of infinite pure Consciousness.

Like a whirling lit incense stick appears as a solid circle of light, Consciousness reverberating everywhere within the infinity of itself appears as form and phenomena. All the forms and phenomena you are experiencing right now are the display of the frequencies of the Aliveness of your own unbounded Awareness. They are the expressed appearance of the universal qualities of your own personhood.

The human being is not only the expressed appearance of the totality of Consciousness at a point, it is the vehicle that Consciousness creates in order to experience and unfold the fullness of itself. The depth, vastness and clarity of Consciousness are unlimited. In its perpetual process of experiencing itself, it is ever refining, ever burnishing, ever polishing its experience of itself. Consciousness is ever in the process of unfolding more of itself to itself. Like a pearl that becomes more lustrous the more it is polished, Consciousness becomes brighter and brighter the more clearly it experiences the flow of itself through individual appearance.

The by-product of Consciousness experiencing itself more deeply is the universal reality of the apparent individual body being experienced more clearly. Your nervous system is the individualized expression of the total aliveness of Consciousness awake within itself. Just as the ocean is shallow closer to shore and deeper in the middle, even though it is the same water, the same one Consciousness can experience itself more deeply through one individual and less deeply through another, depending upon the degree of refinement of the nervous system.

Anyone can have experiences of the divine, to some degree, but that degree of divine experience can only be permanently maintained on the surface level of life through a nervous system that is holistically refined and in balance.

In Unity Consciousness, the experiencer, the process of experiencing, and experience, are all one wholeness of total Being. Everything is Consciousness, and it is all my SELF. Yet, as the perspective deepens and perception refines, a greater clarity of the subtler levels of the total flow of Consciousness begins to emerge. Perception refines to experience the refined flows of Intelligence in the *Experiencer,* that give rise to the flows of creative intelligence in the *Process of Experiencing*, which gives rise to the *Experience* of the physical world appearance. The Experience of the physical world is an elaboration of the flows of universal Intelligence in the Process of Experiencing, which is an elaboration of the subtle reverberations of pure Knowing in the silence of the Experiencer.

In the language of physics, the universe could be said to be the expressed appearance of quantum field interactions, and those quantum field interactions could be said to be expressions of the fluctuations in the quantum vacuum. The quantum vacuum, the quantum field level, and the physical level of life can be likened to Consciousness as the Experiencer, the process of Experiencing, and the Experience itself.

This is directly experienced as the total reality of the SELF in Unity Consciousness—not just as an objective mathematical construct conceptualized by the individual mind conditioned by the false identification with the objects of appearance.

THE VED

The total flow of all the reverberations, vibrations and frequency densities of Consciousness in the perpetual experience of itself, is called the Ved. These reverberations are Consciousness' own narrative of itself, and include the total range of its structure, qualities and functions. They are the flows of pure energy and Intelligence that propel, orchestrate and appear as all life. They are the reverberations of pure Truth, pure Memory, pure Knowledge. They are absolute and eternal and form the basis of all apparent existence. They are the frequencies of the universal Personality of Infinite Consciousness.

These flows of universal Intelligence have been cognized by enlightened seers throughout time. The Vedic literature of India, and other ancient scriptures, are written records of these cognitions. However, on the deepest level, the true Ved is the flow of Consciousness and can only be known by Consciousness, not by the mind or the written word. Translations and commentaries on the Vedas can only provide an incomplete vision of what Ved really is. Even so, due to the tradition of oral recitation passed down through the generations, a good degree of its effect has been preserved.

The four principle Vedas (Rig, Sama, Yajur and Atharva) are expressions of the frequencies of Intelligence of the flow of Consciousness. Rig Veda expresses the wholeness of Consciousness as the oneness of Experiencer, the process of Experiencing and all Experience. The Sama, Yajur and Atharva are the expressions of the frequencies of Intelligence within the modes of Consciousness as the Experiencer *(Knower)*, the process of Experiencing *(Knowing)*, and the Experience *(Known)*. They correspond to the laws governing the quantum vacuum state, the quantum field level, and the physical level of life, respectively.

The initial reverberations of knowing within the *Knower*, which are the primal structuring dynamics of creation (akin to virtual particles of the quantum vacuum), are expressed in the sounds of Sama Veda. The lively flows of pure Intelligence inherent in the process of *Knowing* (quantum field level), are expressed in the sounds of Yajur Veda. The impulses of creative intelligence and laws of nature responsible for the appearance and functioning of the body and universe (the *Known*) are expressed in the sounds of Atharva Veda.

These sounds are the reverberations of the universal reality of your personhood, and the eternal record of the frequencies of Intelligence that form the blueprint of the universe, creation after creation. Your body is the image created by the flow of Consciousness experiencing itself, and it is the central point of all the frequencies and reverberations of universal Intelligence creating the appearance of the universe.

These flows of universal Intelligence are the same quantum field mechanics and laws of nature investigated by physicists, only directly experienced in refined Unity Consciousness as the flows of your SELF. It is not an understanding, an intuition, a sensory perception, or something experienced in a deep meditative state. It is the flow of Consciousness' own experience of itself and is the all-time reality of life in this state.

As these flows of Intelligence begin to awaken in the body, they can initially be experienced as extremely powerful energy surges, and as the enlivenment of universal aspects of personality. The body and nervous system need to be systematically and scientifically cultured and refined over a considerable length of time for experience and perception to be clear and stable. When these flows of Consciousness are integrated into the mind, body and perceptions, true cognition of the Veda is possible. Vedic cognition is Consciousness' clear experience of the universal flows of cosmic Intelligence inherent in its process of being conscious of itself that create, control and appear as the universe. It is the direct perception of the universal Personality of Godhead—the universal aspect of your own personality.

≈≈≈

CHAPTER TWELVE

WITHIN THE FLOW

FROM POTENTIALITY TO EXPRESSED APPEARANCE

When you read this next section, don't try to understand it intellectually. It does not need to be understood by the mind. Its reality can only be directly perceived and experienced by Awakened Consciousness. It cannot be adequately described in words. Read with innocent relaxed alertness and attention, but without too much intellect. It is written to help rekindle the memory of the finer internal dynamics of Consciousness in the inner Self, not to provide personal intellectual knowledge. When innocently heard by open, simple awareness, the cosmic levels of Intelligence that appear as the body and world become enlivened, and this can give rise to finer degrees of comprehension, perception and experience.

As an ocean has many levels of pressure, light and temperature depending upon its depth, Consciousness has levels of density and intensity in the expanse of its infinity. As a pebble dropped into a still pond creates distinct ripples, Consciousness falling back upon itself to know itself creates innumerable waves and frequencies of Intelligence throughout its ocean of infinity.

Prior to the finest impulse of relative expression lies a level where universal Intelligence is powerful, vibrant and alive. It is found at the point of the transformation of pure Intelligence into creative intelligence. It is the warmed-up intensity of alive boundless Being just before its apparent differentiation into specific waves of energy and intelligence. It is the subtle motionless motion of the initial impulse of pure experiencing present in Consciousness as it falls back upon itself and instantaneously expands in the recognition of its own infinity. It is the silence of pure Consciousness open and awake within itself to its reverberant initial impulse of Knowing and Being.

This intensely vibrant stirring of Consciousness is a perpetual reverberating hum of alive Silence. It is the all-powerful, eternal field of pure potentiality of the infinite ocean of Consciousness. It is the source of all the streams of creative intelligence that create, uphold and appear as all life and existence. It is pure Consciousness fully awake within itself, vibrant and alive with infinite possibility.

This alive wholeness of pure Being is the clear wakeful alertness of your own silent, pure Awareness, when unbounded and free from all impressions, with the unrestricted capacity to move deeply within itself to explore the finer flows of the supreme might of its total reality. This alive, energetic, eternal field of pure Energy and Intelligence is generating the impulses of creativity that are actively creating the appearance of everything all around you right now, including your own mind and body.

When Awareness clearly hears the following descriptions of itself, beyond mind and emotions, it can begin to open to more of its infinite depth and clarity. Its inner fabric of pure Being and Knowing becomes more awake and alive. Opening to the flow of itself, perpetually resonating everywhere within the wholeness of its omnipresence, its memory of its infinite creative power is stirred.

Like a soaked seed of total knowledge, ready to sprout, the unmanifest seed of ripened pure Consciousness, moving deeply within itself, swells in infinite creative possibility, revealing more of its effulgent Aliveness and divine dynamics of pure Knowing. It moves within itself from its unmanifest field of Silent unboundedness, to a vibrant field of pure potentiality, to an even more dynamic and alive, superfluid energetic flow of creative intelligence capable of spawning the appearance of the universe out of itself, at the slightest intention.

The perpetual pull and push of its collapse to a point within itself and its simultaneous expansion to its infinity creates a dynamic churning motion in the boundless ocean of Consciousness. This constant churning motion produces a superfluid nectar of vibrant potentiality and possibility. A fine flow of effervescent pure Life, effulgent with divine light and alive bliss, it is the causal incentive inherent in Consciousness stimulating its pure energy and Intelligence to flow in lively impulses of creativity.

The infinite creative power latent within the unboundedness of pure Awareness becomes unleashed in an upsurge of exquisite joy, delight, fullness, and alive, electric excitation throughout the whole field of infinity. The primal structuring dynamics of creation inherent in the flow of Consciousness awakens. The motivational forces behind all thinking, knowing, feeling and experiencing, are activated. The finest impulses of pure power and Intelligence in the ocean of pure Consciousness rise in dynamic frequency-waves of infinite creativity, and in tidal waves of Divine Bliss, flow in the appearance of creation.

THE DEEPENING FLOW

The constant churning motion of the infinite ocean of Consciousness, flowing in waves of infinite possibility, is the cause of the appearance of life on all levels of creation. Like the nourishment from the mother providing energy and nutrition to the fetus, this superfluid flow of pure divine energy, invigorates, enlivens and nourishes all the levels of cosmic Intelligence responsible for creating and sustaining the appearance of the universe.

This divine nutriment is the primal bond of creation, binding together the absolute non-changing pure Being and the ever-changing appearance of life into one wholeness. It maintains the integrity of the individual ego sense, on all levels of life, within the unboundedness of universal Being; without this, creation would not be possible. It is the finest product of pure bliss produced in the perpetual motion of Consciousness knowing itself, and the underlying basis of all perception and experience. Opening to this level of flow is the prerequisite for the clear Refined Perception of the underlying divine mechanics of creation.

Within the wholeness of the unbounded reality of your total Being, there is a perpetual superfluid flow of divine Bliss. It is continually nourishing and balancing the cosmic Intelligence at the universal level of your mind/body, creating and upholding all perception and experience. It stimulates cosmic Intelligence to flow in individual appearance, shaping the flows of infinity into the appearance of form. The world around you is the expressed appearance of this flow of divine bliss.

When perception opens to that level, the whole process of creation is seen mirrored in the body. Every single aspect of your body is a frequency of universal Intelligence flowing in waves of individual appearance, nourished by the invigorating streams of pure divine nutrition produced by the motion of Consciousness knowing itself. The clearer the perception becomes, the more bliss and joy is felt throughout the entire being.

The direct experience of some degree of this flow is open to anyone, depending upon the degree of refinement of their nervous system. If you are simple, innocent and open, you may even enjoy a dip into the ocean of joy right now as you continue reading.

Consciousness, perpetually flowing in the knowing of itself,
  flows in waves of bliss

It flows in the process of seeing, feeling, experiencing

It flows in the reading of these words

It is sensed in the Presence all around you

Feel the Aliveness in the space around you...

Be with that alive Presence

It is a lively joy

That Aliveness is the effect of the aliveness of Awareness it-self...
  the activity of Awareness being aware of itself
  the quantum field activity of your own brain
  the cosmic activity of your own mind
  the finest level of your Being,
  fully awake within itself

Be with that Aliveness...
  It is everywhere
  It permeates all objects of perception
  It permeates your body

It flows between your eyes and the page

It is pure Joy

It is the lively flow of universal Intelligence...

   the flow of Consciousness experiencing itself

   the flow of the Joy of Being

   the flow of pure Life

The objects you are experiencing are created by the mind out of the flow of the pure joy of Consciousness, awake and alive within itself. They have distracted you from the true experience of the finer reality of your Being.

Individual mind believes it sees real physical objects, completely unaware that, unconsciously, every split second, its universal Intelligence is creating the images of the world out of the lively flows of the pure joy of Being.

The unconscious universal aspect of your mind shapes the flow of the joy of Being into the images of the world in front of you.

The ocean of Consciousness flows in waves of appearance...

   It flows in waves of bliss

   It flows as the seer, the seeing and the seen

   It flows as Life itself

   It is the flow of the pure Joy of Being...

Pure Awareness, hidden by the objects within it, becomes awake to the subtle joy inherent within itself.

It feels itself, shining more brightly from within every object...

flowing in the seeing, reading, thinking, feeling

flowing between your eyes and their objects

flowing in the appearance of your body and the world

creating the appearance of all objects

See the seer seeing...

    observe the mind reading

    feel the feelings feeling

    be the Awareness that is aware

Seeing the seer awakens Awareness to the knowing of itself...

    a wave of joy arises

    clarity, aliveness, freedom and joy are awakening

    the boundlessness of Being is enlivened,

    reverberating in lively joy

The whole field of Presence around you is warming up...

    Its Stillness becomes more alive

    filling the surrounding space

    Its wholeness permeates the surroundings

Perception takes in the whole field of observation...

    the light in the room brightens

    the pure light of Awareness intensifies

    penetrating your perceptions

    shining the objects to a finer glow

Increasing alertness...

> *clarity*
>
> *spaciousness*
>
> *smoothness*
>
> *freedom*
>
> *lightness*
>
> *joy*

Flowing in streams of perceiving, feeling and experiencing

Pure Being, seeing its SELF seeing itself, flows in waves of Joy...

> *destroying doubt,*
>
> *fear,*
>
> *all negative thoughts and moods*

> *creating happiness,*
>
> *flowing in waves of pure happiness*

Happiness is the result of the experiencer experiencing itself in the objects of experience.

Happiness is universal Joy experiencing itself through individual appearance.

There is only the pure Joy of Being...

> *the light of pure Awareness*
>
> *fully awake*

flowing in the knowing of itself,
in sheer delight

A grand wholeness surrounds and pervades everything...
a blissful wholeness of alive Presence
a lively Presence full of pure potentiality,
reverberating in waves of joy and delight

Particles of joy are dancing in the Presence all around you...
dancing in the seeing of these words
dancing within every object you see
dancing in your thoughts
dancing in your feelings

dancing in your body
dancing in your bones

creating the appearance of your body
creating the appearance of the universe

All objects of perception are ripples of delight, waves of Joy...
the entire space around you is alive with life
the air is alive with life energy
your entire being is alive with excitement

The body, relaxing its tension, shaking off its tightness and resistance, becomes more alive...

lighter

more fluid

feeling more joy

It surrenders to the simple peaceful joy that is here right now in this timeless moment...

breath is finer

head is lighter

Subtle, alive life energy flows throughout the whole body...

It feels lighter

more expanded

as if porous

boundless

more alive and energetic

almost electric...

"My body is alive with joyful excitation."

The intelligence of the body awakens in celebration...

flowing in bubbling joy, happiness and laughter

The body is the image of lively universal Joy...

flowing in individual appearance

flowing in bliss

Hearing itself, Consciousness remembers its blissful Joy...

activating endorphins in the brain

creating alive, energetic bliss

A surge of joyful energy and excitation is felt everywhere...

opening perception to subtler levels of joyful life

The light of Consciousness smiles and shines more brightly...

awakening to its superfluid flow of the Joy of Being

"The space around me is alive with joy! There is a lightness, fullness, expansion, and flow of energetic, alive joy throughout the whole of my being...

"How could I have been so lost in all my thoughts, moods, concepts and perceptions and missed this lively joy of being here now?"

Everything is perfect

Everything is beautiful

Everything is bliss

There is not a care in the world.

Close the eyes and enjoy...

DIVINE NECTAR

If you have been reading this with simple open innocence, some finer degree of experience is likely beginning to open. You are getting a glimpse into the abstract flow of Consciousness in its process of experiencing itself. You are becoming more awake to the refined flow of energy and intelligence at the quantum field level of your brain—the cosmic dimension of your own mind. Pure Awareness is awakening to its process of creating.

If perception is refined enough, the churning action produced by the flow of Consciousness within itself may peak in the production of a fluid-like, light-matter substance of vibrantly alive, divine nectar that drips from the back of the pallet onto the tongue. It mixes with the saliva in the mouth creating electric joy and bliss, and when swallowed, passes down the esophagus through the stomach, into the small intestine. In the villi of the intestines, it is ingested by the subtle levels of intelligence that govern the functions of the body, creating waves of energetic aliveness, ecstasy, euphoria and bliss in every organ, cell and atom throughout the body.

The subtle levels of intelligence that partake of this divine substance, called soma, are the same quantum fields of cosmic Intelligence that are responsible for creating and maintaining the appearance of the world and universe.

The finest product of the quantum field level of your own brain and digestive system is feeding the cosmic Intelligence that is creating the appearance of the world around you. The universal reality of your own mind and body is stimulated and enlivened, and the entire life within and around you is nourished, revitalized and renewed.

When this level of refinement is established, the cosmic laws of nature conducting the universe are enlivened and offer constant support to your life. Desires and actions are the desires and actions of nature and naturally become more spontaneous, positive, evolutionary and easily fulfilled.

The subtle aspect of the human body is like a cosmic refinery. It produces the divine nectar of pure soma for the nourishment of cosmic Intelligence to create and uphold the vast expanse of the appearance of the universe. In return, individual life gains greater enrichment, happiness, and support from nature. *This is the symbiotic relationship between man and nature, between the individual and the universe, between the human and the divine, between creation and its source.*

This divine soma is the subtlest aspect of relative existence. In its raw state it is latent everywhere within all of nature. In its refined state it is actively nourishing the finest cosmic quantum field levels of the brain responsible for perception, feeling, thought and action. These quantum field levels are the universal flows of pure Intelligence responsible for the creation of all apparent forms and phenomena on all levels of creation.

Every quality and frequency of universal Intelligence, at every level within the infinity of Consciousness, is nourished and invigorated. They become vibrantly alive and alert in complete readiness, eagerly awaiting the subtlest command. With the faintest intention, the cosmic aspect of mind creates and recreates the appearance of the world and universe out of that vast dynamism of infinite possibilities within the unbounded reality of pure Consciousness—just as imagination creates forms out of the clouds floating in the sky.

In its process of experiencing itself, Consciousness, remaining pure and unmodified, appears as the form and phenomena of the universe. In the reverberant frequencies and intensities of energy and intelligence within its flow, Consciousness is the ego, intellect, mind, space, energy, light, fluidity, solidity, and all possible combinations of the qualities of its infinite Intelligence that appear as all creation.

It is all one superfluid flow of infinite pure Consciousness. It is all your SELF. At the finest universal level of your mind, you are creating the appearance of the world around you continuously, every split second, in the timeless instant of Now, even though you may be completely unconscious of it.

The product of the perpetual flow of Consciousness conscious of itself, and the essential stimulus for creation, is soma. It is everywhere. As such, some degree of the divine nectar of pure soma can be experienced by anyone, enlightened or not. Soma is the ultimate cause of any experience of spontaneous joy or a natural high that may seem to happen for no apparent reason. It is also the cause of the blissful energy experienced in the creative process, as it is the stimulus for the creative flow itself. It nourishes the finest feelings of love and intimacy beyond all sentiment and emotion. It enlivens the intelligence responsible for clear thinking, uncolored perception, and right action. It neutralizes imbalances and past negative impressions and stresses, revitalizes the body, and enlivens the positive evolutionary qualities of life.

However, very few people in this age experience the production of soma in its refined purity. Even those who have Awakened to being Consciousness itself, may seldom experience the pure flow of this divine nectar. It is no wonder that life has been lived virtually devoid of clear refined perception and the true experience of the divine reality that it actually is. The degree to which the nervous system is refined, and Consciousness can clearly experience its process of being conscious of itself, is the degree to which true divine life can be lived through individual appearance.

At the most refined level, the solid physical appearance of the world and universe is found to be the finest, most precious expression of Consciousness. It is the finest level of the internal dynamics of Consciousness, and the display of pure divine Intelligence in flow. It only appears to be a solid physical reality from the perspective of individual mind, unawakened to the true reality of the fullness of the SELF.

From the perspective of refined Unity Consciousness, all levels of creation are experienced simultaneously, superimposed one within the other, and they are all the flow of the wholeness of your own SELF. The universe is the expressed appearance of the frequencies of Intelligence in the unbounded field of infinite potentiality—the perpetual flow of Consciousness conscious of itself. It is the creation of the universal intelligence at the finest level of your own mind.

QUANTUM FIELD THINKING

At the finest relative level, your mind is universal. It is the quantum field reality of the brain, and it is instantaneously creating and recreating the images of the world around you. It is in the gap between individual mind and absolute unbounded pure Being. It can be accessed to some degree, by anyone who experiences clear transcendental consciousness. It is a silent, yet vibrant level of boundless potentiality of alive intelligence prior to thoughts, emotions and perceptions. It is responsible for the manifestation of your thoughts and desires. A thought consciously held at this finest level of mind is instantaneously fulfilled at that level, and in time and space, will eventually manifest on the surface of life to the degree it can through that nervous system.

Quantum field thinking means having conscious access to, at least some degree, of this universal field of infinite potentiality at the finest level of the mind. Access to this level can be gradually opened through the regular practice of effortless transcendental deep meditation techniques. Through regular transcending to deep inner silence, peace, expansion and bliss, the awareness begins to open to this level. Through repeated experience, this level becomes more and more infused into the nature of the mind and nervous system. As a result, individual life gains more support from nature's intelligence. Thoughts, feelings and actions become naturally more positive, evolutionary and life-supporting. Desires are fulfilled more quickly, and with less effort. Life is spontaneously lived more in tune with natural law.

It is from this level that siddhis (special abilities) can be experienced. The word "siddhi" means perfection. Siddhis are the result of the opening of specific channels of the coordination between the mind and body while functioning from the transcendental level. They are not necessarily an indication of awakened Consciousness. It is possible to be far from Awakening, or even from a balanced holistic development, and still have some specific channels of perfection open. On the other hand, one can be very clearly awakened and have no experience of siddhis at all.

Experiences of siddhis can even be a barrier to enlightenment if the first shift to cosmic Consciousness has not been firmly established. They can be so enticing, that they can create an attachment to experiences, strengthening the individual ego sense—which is in the opposite direction of awakening. Siddhi experiences, however charming, are just experiences. Attachment to experiences can cause the real awakening to *being* Consciousness itself (the source of all experience) to be missed.

It is better not to get too impressed with flowery descriptions of subtle levels, divine experiences, or siddhi abilities. Some people can have a measure of finer perception or special abilities developed through practice or past effort. But if the clear awakening to *being* unbounded pure Awareness has not happened, there will still be a separate individual ego taking ownership of it, and the perspective will be incomplete. Awakening to the unbounded reality of your total Being is far more important, and the essential beginning for the true divine unfoldment of life. From the perspective of awakened Consciousness, phenomenal life is relatively insignificant.

There are certain mental techniques for a well-rounded development, that if practiced properly, can be holistically beneficial for anyone, whether awakened or not. Sanyama techniques are methods of effortless focused thinking utilizing specific sutras (subtle thoughts or sounds) practiced from the field of transcendental Consciousness. They help to refine the nervous system and perception and improve the general quality of life.

When practiced properly, these techniques can produce a powerfully beneficial, evolutionary effect throughout the whole field of Consciousness, as they enliven the quantum field Intelligence at the basis of the mind where everything is intimately connected. There are many things that can be done to improve our lives and the life of society, but those who have access to the deeper universal quantum field levels of the mind and brain have the ability to positively affect the consciousness of everyone at the deepest and most profound level.

Sanyama techniques are meant for the unfoldment of finer levels of the divine fullness of Consciousness. After clear Awakening, the practice of sanyama helps to infuse pure Consciousness into the mind and body, further refining perception and holistic unfoldment. Life then begins to take on more of the true character of the divine reality that it actually is.

Those who have awakened to refined Unity Consciousness have an even greater beneficial effect on the consciousness of the world. In this state "you *are* the world". You are unbounded, universal Consciousness, and everything is your SELF. When perception in that state has refined enough to experience the divine impulses of Intelligence that are creating the appearance of the universe, the ability to influence the life of society in a positive direction is greatly increased. It is a great service to the world to be able to think, act and live from this superfluid level of quantum field Intelligence.

The evolutionary force of the flow of divine creative intelligence is moving through all of us all the time whether we realize it or not. When we are not consciously opening ourselves to its influence through a systematic spiritual practice, progress in the direction of greater perfection and joy in life may not be as fast.

Ultimately, whether we are awake to it or not, there is only that quantum field of infinite potentiality of the flow of pure Intelligence. All thoughts originate from that level. The quality of our thoughts and moods determines the quality of our life. A depressed thought, feeling or memory creates depression, an angry thought creates anger, a happy thought creates happiness. We are very powerful beings and should be awake to the quality of the thoughts and moods we are dominantly entertaining and projecting into our environment. It is those thoughts and moods that will surely become manifest in our life and affect the lives of those around us.

THE LIVING REALITY

Divine Intelligence is everywhere within everything. It *is* everything. The clear perception of this reality unfolds gradually over time as Consciousness awakens more clearly, and as the nervous system refines and the flow of infinity becomes more infused into the mind and body. The solid physical body-idea begins to melt. The body feels lighter and more fluid, almost as if it is porous and transparent.

The universal quantum field flows of Intelligence responsible for creating and performing the functions of the body open to the perception. The cosmic life in the body awakens. The finer, more beautiful, universal, divine qualities of your total personhood awaken. They are simple, innocent, pure qualities—frequencies of the flow of the boundless joy of pure Being. They are unbounded, fluid and free. They are the same universal laws of nature responsible for creating and upholding the appearance of the universe.

Everyone is a unique configuration of these same universal qualities. Your personhood has been universal all along, only the perception has not been refined enough to experience that reality. When awakened in your body, any specific combination of those universal qualities can be instantly experienced. They become so fluid in the body that they can assume the configuration of whatever personality you think of, or are in the vicinity of, at the moment. The qualities of your personality instantaneously shift to the qualities of personality of those around you. You literally become what you see. This is because the qualities of your personality are not individual—they are universal and always have been. The body is cosmic. (This is why it is important to be conscious of the company we keep, and what we put our attention on).

On the level of Being, SELF is everything everywhere, only now, Consciousness is more familiar with the finer flows of its own Self knowing. These fine flows of Consciousness are the qualities of universal Intelligence that create and appear as form and phenomena and are the universal reality of your own total Being. The universal reality of individual personhood is always there, regardless of the life situation or circumstance. It is expressed in the appearance of all life everywhere. People, plants, animals, the whole of nature and the entire cosmos, are the expressed appearance of the qualities of the cosmic aspect of your own person.

The interactions that take place in the collective consciousness of society are the interactions of the cosmic aspect of your own personality. Your thoughts are the individualized notions of the play of cosmic Intelligence. Cosmic Intelligence has been thinking, feeling and acting through you all along. Only due to conditioning, you have taken those thoughts and actions to be your own and have suffered the pains and restrictions of being falsely identified with something you are not. You have mistaken yourself to be just an individual person even though you are unbounded pure Awareness. Your thoughts, emotions and actions are propelled by the flow of universal Intelligence found at every point within that unboundedness. Whose thoughts, feelings and actions are they, in reality?

The content of thought may seem individualized and different for everyone, but *the impulses of intelligence* giving rise to all personal thought, feeling, perception and action are cosmic and universal. Those impulses are the flow of universal Intelligence experienced at the point of individual appearance. In truth, there is no such thing as a separate individual thought or action. The effect of every thought, feeling and action is felt everywhere throughout creation. You are the individualized appearance of universal Intelligence. Individual life is orchestrated by universal Intelligence. When unawake to the true reality of our total Being, we are like pawns in the cosmic chess game of creation.

In the state of refined Unity Consciousness, cosmic Intelligence flows through and as every perception and experience. The SELF sees its universal divine frequencies and flavors of pure Intelligence flowing in the appearance of form and phenomena. Its wholeness is in every frequency, flavor and form of its flow. Sensory perception is wholeness flowing in frequencies of knowing, and as such, the fullness of every sense is contained within each sense. Feeling, touching and tasting are clearly felt in everything seen or heard. All the qualities of life around you are qualities of your own personality and divine flows of the boundless reality of your Being.

Each frequency of the flow is a unique flavor and specific quality of bliss. The infinite variety of configurations, combinations and interactions of these frequencies (of cosmic Intelligence in the appearance of the world and universe) fill the wholeness of Being with wave after wave of divine fullness and bliss. Everything is vibrant and alive with bliss. It is all one life flowing in the appearance of form. You *are* that Life. All qualities are superimposed, one within the other, flowing within the wholeness of perpetual SELF knowing.

Rather than being an area of study or intellectual investigation, the quantum field mechanics of the universe are found to be the interactions of the finest boundless universal levels of your own person. Rather than being esoteric knowledge, hymns or chants, the Vedas are experienced in your body and everywhere in the world around you as the frequencies of the flow of your own Consciousness.

The most intimate universal level of your own heart and soul is displayed right in front of you through your perceptions as all the forms and phenomena of experience. What was experienced as a separate physical world and universe, is now revealed to be the cosmic reality of your own personhood, and the finest, most intimate aspect of your Being. Absolute pure Being has opened to the finest relative level of its cosmic heart and has found it to be everywhere within every perception on the surface of life.

Life on all levels is the flow of your own fine feelings. The feelings of others are felt as your own and a deep compassion is felt for all. And yet, the invincible wholeness of the total flow of pure Being is so all-encompassing that its fullness never diminishes regardless of what is happening in individual and collective life. Instead, it is found to be ever-increasing in its fullness through the experience of living. The divine reality of life is experienced as it actually is. You feel as though you are the parent of everyone and everything, nourishing and protecting your children. All of nature and all beings are your intimate family. They are your own SELF.

Consciousness flows in divine love and joy, unsullied by emotion, thought or phenomena. All things are conceived out of pure Love/Bliss and are the expressed appearance of the flow of divine love and joy. The heart is not individual—it is a universal cosmic heart. All life is the expression of the pulsation of that universal heart.

It is not that you have love for all beings and all things, but that the finest level of your Being *is* the divine flow of pure Love/Bliss out of which everything is composed. Universal Love is pure Love without attachment, without a lover or a beloved. It is the unconditioned flow of pure Love itself. Universal Love is the finest flow of Consciousness experiencing itself in the appearance of creation.

From the perspective of the physical appearance of life, everything remains much the same. Only now, the finer values of the wholeness of your total Being are known and lived through all perception and experience. You still have personal preferences, but simultaneously, the wholeness of the total flow of life, beyond all preferences, dominates. You still have human emotions, and yet simultaneously, sublime divine universal pure feeling dominates.

Life is experienced as the flow of love, compassion, gratitude, reverence, fullness and bliss. The finest levels of feeling and perception are appreciated on such a refined level that words are incapable of expressing their divine exquisiteness. The ordinary experience of life in refined Unity Consciousness is, at times, almost too beautiful to bear.

When that finest level is opened to perception and lived, a most exquisite experience of divine joy becomes the dominant reality of life. It is the stable reality of your Being and is found within everything everywhere. The finest, most tender level of divine feeling has merged with the invincible light of absolute Being, and remains untouched by the circumstances of life, regardless of how difficult. The innermost divine core of the heart of Being is experienced on the surface of life in all form and phenomena.

The act of perceiving and experiencing is found to be the eternal flow of the ocean of the divine love and joy of pure Being. The finest level of the universal heart of Being shines through, and as, everything everywhere.

From that perspective, life is smooth, harmonious and conflict free. Every thought, word and action come from the deepest level of Being and have only the best interest of others and the world in mind. It is not possible to entertain negative or profane thoughts, feelings or actions. It is not possible to purposely hurt anyone or anything, because it would be hurting your own Self.

However, others (who may not yet be viewing from the same unbounded perspective and refined perception) still see you as a separate individual person with your own ideas, opinions and ego. From that level, apparent conflict may still arise. You experience the "other" as your own SELF, and are intimately aware of their feelings, whether positive or negative. You can only feel great compassion for them, even if they may have negative perceptions, judgments and feelings towards you. When unawake to its true total reality, conditioned and tainted by the stress of world appearance, the false sense of individual self, not only remains in conflict within, but with its own SELF that appears as the form of others. We can only see what we are.

What we see and experience is a reflection of the degree of refinement of our own nervous system. The world is an extension of our own body and the expressed appearance of the quantum field reality of our brain and nervous system. The more refined the nervous system, the more refined the perception; the more refined the perception, the more the environment reflects that refined perception. We can only be what we are.

Ultimately, there is only one Being, one Heart, one Body, one Life. Everyone is an expression of that one Life and ultimately is that Oneness. Oneness is here now and only needs to be awakened in you. It is the universal reality of your life and the source of all knowledge, perception and experience.

The physical body is a body of impressions that has arisen due to past identification and conditioning. But, the real universal body is the divine flow of the total Intelligence inherent in the process of Consciousness being awake within itself. The physical body is the image created in that process, at that point of appearance, and the vehicle for Consciousness to unfold the divine fullness of itself.

In refined Unity Consciousness, the flow of divine Intelligence is awakened and lived. But there is something more. The ultimate causal force which drives the flow of Consciousness and Intelligence is not yet experienced. There is a deeper level of pure Power and Divinity that is the cause of the universal sense of Being and the flow of cosmic Intelligence. This ultimate force cannot be known until the universal SELF disappears, and all apparent existence disappears with it.

≈≈≈

PART IV

BEYOND SELF

CHAPTER THIRTEEN

THE REALITY OF NOTHING

WHAT IS NOTHING?

Pure Consciousness is the timeless, eternal present moment of Now. Everything that has ever happened, however many billions of years ago, or anything that will ever happen in the future, happens in the eternal present moment of Now. The timeless Now is the eternal universal sense of Being that is found to be your own unbounded Self in the state of Cosmic Consciousness. That timeless pure Being awakens to itself as everything everywhere, in the state of Unity Consciousness. From that perspective, everything is my SELF. Everything is Consciousness. Everything that has ever happened has happened in Consciousness and is Consciousness in appearance. Consciousness is all there is.

But what is Consciousness? Where does it come from? What is its origin?

Without Consciousness, there would be no senses to pick up the electromagnet signals in the environment, and no brain to transform those signals into something meaningful. There would be no time or space for anything to happen in. There would be no air, light, water or earth. There would be no electromagnetic signals and no environment. There would be no world or universe. There would be no one to experience anything and nothing to experience. There would be no existence.

There would be Nothing.

Is Nothing the source of Consciousness?

Is Nothing a something?

The concept of Nothing, not-Being, or Nothingness is not new. It has been a serious topic of debate by philosophers for thousands of years. Many theologians believe that God created the universe out of Nothing. Nothingness is the very foundation of some Eastern religions. Quantum Physicists have concluded that, at the most fundamental level of the universe, there is really nothing there. It is a void, a vacuum.

Is Nothing a reality? If there is something that can be called "nothing", then what is Nothing? What is the Nothingness out of which Consciousness and the universe comes into being?

Nothingness is a reality, though not in the way the mind is capable of imagining. It is the pure source/essence of Awareness itself.

Before there can be a true appreciation of the majesty of the Divinity that creates and appears as the universe, another major Awakening occurs. It is a shift to a state beyond the universal SELF, to the primal source of Consciousness itself—to Nothingness. This state has been called by many names: Beyond SELF, Beyond God, Brahman Consciousness, No-SELF, Not-Being, and Nothingness.

The term "Nothingness" is used because there is absolutely no existence there. It is prior to the sense of Being because the universal, unbounded, absolute, unchanging sense of Being and existing itself has been transcended. There is no SELF there. The unbounded sense of SELF that is everything everywhere in Unity Consciousness has completely disappeared— and along with it, all existence disappears.

This section will undoubtedly be puzzling to the mind, but just remain simple and innocent and allow the words to flow through without trying to conceptualize. The true shift to Nothingness itself can only happen to fully Awakened Consciousness. Intellectual understanding or desire will not get you there. As you continue to read, let go of the need to know anything. Remain settled in the peace, stillness and Presence that is within, and around you, right now.

THE DISAPPEARANCE OF THE UNIVERSE

When everything is my SELF, existence is a reality. The body, world and universe exist because they are all my SELF, which is the only thing that is real. This is the direct experience in Unity Consciousness. But when the SELF disappears, the viewpoint is completely different. In the "state" of Nothingness, there is no sense of Being, individual, cosmic or universal, to know or experience anything. There is only pure Nothingness. When there is no SELF appearing as everything, there is no everything. When the SELF disappears, all existence disappears.

Nothingness is prior to the sense of Being where the universe is experienced prior to its existence. Before the flow of cosmic Intelligence that creates the appearance of the universe, there is no universe, no creation and no existence. In this state, the world appears the same, but it has no existence whatsoever. From that perspective, *nothing has ever been created*. The Nothingness prior to existence is directly experienced everywhere within the appearance of existence. It is being the universe *prior* to its existence.

This is not the same as when the sense of being an individual separate self disappears after the shift to Cosmic Consciousness. In the shift to Nothingness, it is the universal sense of Being that disappears. The unbounded field of pure Awareness in which everything exists is found not to be the ultimate source of all existence after all. From the perspective beyond Consciousness, there is no existence.

In Cosmic Consciousness, there is a sense of detachment from the body and world. In the state of Nothingness, there is no detachment from the world. It is not possible to be detached from something that does not exist. The world, universe and all existence are experienced, from this perspective, as the non-existence of Nothingness in appearance. All existence *is* Nothingness. There is no SELF, and there is no everything. There is only non-existent pure Nothingness appearing as all existence.

In the first Awakening to unbounded, absolute pure Awareness, the world exists within my Self. In the second Awakening, the world *is* my SELF. In the third Awakening, the world is non-existent, because there is no SELF. From this perspective, the world is made of Nothingness, and is therefore, directly experienced as being non-existent. Something made of pure non-existence cannot be said to exist. This is not an intellectual understanding, conviction or belief. There is no one there to believe or experience anything because all sense of self, whether individual or cosmic, has been transcended. It is the state of Nothingness.

Nothingness cannot be said to be pure Awareness, nor can it be said to not be pure Awareness. It is not Consciousness, yet it cannot be said to be non-Consciousness. It is not Being, yet it is not non-Being. It cannot be said to be the Absolute because the Absolute has existence. Nothingness is beyond all existence, manifest and unmanifest; yet absolute pure Being and all existence appears within it. No "one" can know it or experience it. Only It can know itself.

This may sound perplexing, but that is only because words cannot convey the reality. It is something that can only be known by Itself. It is actually the simplest, most all-comprehensive state of complete freedom, strength and self-sufficiency. It includes all attributes of the previous states of Consciousness, yet there are no states within it. It is all-inclusive pure Nothingness. Everything is non-existent Nothingness in the appearance of existence. Yet everything remains the same as it is now, only Being has awakened to the source and total expanse of itself beyond all existence.

Pure Nothingness is beyond all concepts of God as the creator, maintainer and destroyer. It is completely on its own level while including all levels. It is eternal and uncreated, yet all creation appears within it in a state prior to its existence. Existence, made from the material of pure non-existence, cannot exist. What was never really created, cannot truly exist. It can only *appear* to exist.

Logically, it is not possible for something to be created out of Nothing. If something is created out of Nothing, then it is not something: it is Nothing *in the appearance of something*. The ultimate reality of something created out of Nothing is Nothing, not something. $0 + 0 = 0$, not 1. This is the ultimate formula for the Theory of Everything—everything is Nothing in appearance.

THE ARISING OF THE UNIVERSE

How does everything arise from Nothing and still remain Nothing in the appearance of everything?

Inherent within the silence of Nothingness, there is a latent tendency, or subtle unmanifest intention, to know and to Be. This subtle intention is hidden by the appearance of existence. From the perspective of Nothingness, there is no sequential unfoldment of creation in space and time. There is no such thing as space or time. There is no perception of the force of evolution and the power driving it. Everything is happening all at once, and yet, nothing is happening at all.

Time and space do not come into play until Consciousness becomes conscious of itself and gives rise to the unbounded sense of Being and universal Mind. Consciousness, awake within itself, gives rise to the flow of Intelligence, and this flow of Intelligence creates the sense of time and space and the appearance of existence from the perspective of mind.

The initial impulse of unmanifest pure intention, hidden deep within timeless pure Nothingness, is the primal cause of the appearance of existence. The whole creation appears, *instantaneously all at once,* in the opening of the Nothingness to its inherent tendency to know and to Be. There are no steps, no progression, no expansion, no evolution from this perspective. Everything is already inherent in, and the image of, the latent intention to Be. It is this latent tendency that stimulates the eternal memory of Consciousness within pure Nothingness, inciting pure Intelligence to flow in waves of creativity and appear as all existence. Yet, on its own level, while appearing as all existence, pure Nothingness remains non-existent.

The state of pure Nothingness does not mean living with the attitude that there is nothing here. It is living the direct experience of being the total field of life prior to existence. The world is not negated or disregarded. It is Nothingness in appearance, which is *absolutely precious.* All apparent levels of Self and creation have been transcended, and life now begins to revel in the discovery of greater fullness and richness of continuing unfoldment.

From the perspective of Nothingness, everything is Nothingness, and all perspectives of Consciousness are included within it. However, at this stage, pure Nothingness has not yet awakened to the true genesis of its own fullness. It is the broadest perspective, but it is not the finest level of perception within that perspective. It is not yet the Ultimate Reality.

REFINED PERCEPTION BEYOND SELF

To whatever degree the nervous system has been refined, perception is experienced from a finer and more comprehensive perspective in the state of Nothingness. Yet initially, the shift to being Nothingness is so powerful that any degree of finer perception previously experienced pales in comparison. The non-existence of everything is so profound that it can overshadow even the finest levels of divine perception. However, after some time in that state, a clearer and deeper value of refined perception can begin to emerge.

Nothingness is not the final stage of enlightenment as expressed in some traditions, although resting in the complete self-sufficiency and equanimity beyond SELF is incredibly profound. As the nervous system acclimatizes to this state and as perception refines, the finest impulses prior to the appearance of creation can begin to be perceived.

From the clear perspective of pure Nothingness, there is no ego sense, no perceptions, thoughts or feelings that can cloud the direct cognition of pure Truth. Prior to this state, it is still possible to get caught in images, feelings, sensations, perceptions and phenomena however subtle, spiritual or divine. But at this point, if the nervous system is sufficiently refined and perception is clear and untainted, it is no longer possible to get caught in phenomena of any kind.

Direct cognition is not on the level of understanding, knowing, feeling or intuition. It is on the level of direct perception of the finest impulse of pure Intention within Nothingness prior to the appearance of existence. Perception refines to perceive the rising wave of the subtlest impulse within Nothingness to know and to Be. This is the finest, yet most powerful level of pure divine energy, that was previously beyond experience.

It is this initial spark of pure divine power that gives rise to Consciousness, Intelligence and Existence. It is hidden deep within Nothingness, beyond the universal sense of Being. It is the primal cause of Consciousness and the divine force that propels pure Intelligence to create, govern and appear as the body, world and universe. The manifest appearance of creation is the form of the formless power of the subtle intention of pure Nothingness to know and to Be.

A far more comprehensive vision of total reality is experienced from this perspective. From the Nothingness—to its latent intention to Be, to the emergence of Consciousness and the flow of pure Intelligence, to the arising of the impulses of intelligence responsible for creating and appearing as the universe—the total range of existence and non-existence is lived. The entire manifest and unmanifest creation is the play and display of the pure power inherent in the latent intention of pure Nothingness to know and to Be. Existence and non-existence do not coexist from this perspective. There is only pure non-existence, and within it resides the power that appears as all existence.

Since there is no sense of even a cosmic SELF, the universal qualities of intelligence that make up the apparent personhood can be more easily recognized on their own level. The finest impulses of intelligence prior to existence have awakened in the body and are experienced throughout the entire field of perception. They are the same universal laws (that create, govern and appear as the form and phenomena of nature and the universe) now experienced from the level of their cause, not their apparent manifestation. Because of this, a certain power is experienced throughout every breath, every word spoken, every movement. This power is invisible to onlookers because its non-existence cannot be accessed by them. The body is the central display of all those qualities of cosmic Intelligence and the access point of the supreme power that impels those laws and qualities of intelligence to perform their functions.

Though a deeper sense of divine peace, joy, self-sufficiency, equanimity, and holiness can be experienced at this stage, perception has not yet opened to the clear experience of the Supreme Divinity that is the ultimate power source causing

Nothingness to become Consciousness, Intelligence and Existence. That pure power source is hidden deep within the Nothingness in the guise of creation, which, from that perspective, is experienced as non-existent. It may be the dawn of pure Divinity, but the sun has not yet risen. In this state, the clear realization is that: *"this is only the beginning"*. At some point that rising fullness and holiness of pure divine power can shed its disguise and burst into clear vision through the surface appearance of life as Supreme Divinity itself.

≈≈≈

CHAPTER FOURTEEN

PURE DIVINITY

THE ULTIMATE MIRACLE

If perception opens to a pivotal point of clarity, another shift in perspective occurs. Nothingness awakens to the true supreme source of infinite power within itself that is the primal motivational force behind Consciousness and all apparent existence. That power source has been disguised in the appearance of existence all along. The sun of divine power that was rising on the horizon of infinity, now shines brightly as the pure power source of Supreme Divinity in all its divine radiance and splendor.

The ultimate force behind Consciousness (and its divine cosmic Intelligence that appears as the body, world and universe) is revealed, and that indescribable supreme light source of pure Divine Radiance becomes the dominant perspective from that moment on.

Beyond existence and nonexistence, hidden deep within the Nothingness, that Supreme Divinity is the initial intention and essential spur to Be. It is the primal cause of everything. It is the original motivating force that drives creation, evolution, destruction, annihilation and recreation. Pure Divinity is the supreme source and cause of all cause and effect. It is eternal and absolute, without beginning or end. It always was and always will be.

That supreme power source has been in the thoughts and on the lips of everyone that has ever lived, if only on the level of faith, belief, disbelief or condemnation. It has been theorized in philosophies and sciences and has been universally acknowledged and sought after in all religions and spiritual traditions. It has been called by many names: God, Universal Mother, Divine Mother, that which cannot be uttered, the Supreme Divinity, the Supreme Lord, and so on.

Although generally conceptualized by the mind as being a Divine entity, Pure Divinity is an unlimited field of pure divine power beyond all concepts and all entities—the power behind Consciousness itself to create, or even conceive of, entities, forms or phenomena. There are no words in any language capable of describing that supreme Divinity. Rare are those who have glimpsed that pure radiant light, more powerful and brilliant than that of millions of suns.

There are countless aspects and qualities of divine intelligence responsible for creating and maintaining the appearance of creation. Each one is so exquisitely majestic and divine, that even a glimpse of one of those qualities in its pure divine flow can be overwhelming. Yet, all those qualities combined cannot compare to the ineffable radiance of the eternal, boundless reality of the pure Supreme Divinity that is the ultimate power source, hidden deep within the Nothingness, beyond the SELF, beyond cosmic intelligence, beyond everything.

This pure Divine Power Source is the generator that sparks the luminescence in the eternal light of unbounded pure Consciousness. It is the initial incentive in the hollowness of the seed of pure Nothingness causing it to sprout into Consciousness and Intelligence, and flower into the appearance of creation.

Life is not the miracle. The real miracle is the incredible Supreme Divine Power that gives life, and appears as, all life. It is the cause, the essence and the whole of the sense of Being, the mind and body, the world and universe, and all existence. It is hidden deep within the alive Presence around you right now.

It is the unseen supreme causal energy force of pure Divine Light that appears as your body and everything all around you.

It is the incredible *Power of Illusion.*

THE SUPREME POWER OF ILLUSION

This Supreme Power of Illusion has been disguised as Consciousness, Intelligence, the universe, everyone and everything, all along. Once this perspective has been revealed, there is no going back. It becomes clear that there was never an individual person evolving towards enlightenment. You have been unbounded pure Consciousness unfolding and awakening to the total divine reality of itself through individual and world appearance all along.

Consciousness is Consciousness due to the subtle impulse inherent in pure Nothingness to know and to Be. That stimulus is pure Supreme Divinity, the ultimate power source and force creating Consciousness and the universal Intelligence that appears as all existence in the first place. It is the true cause of all causes and the supreme source of the source.

There is no distinction between Nothingness and its Supreme divine power, just as there is no distinction between God and the will of God. It is one thing. Yet, without that primal pure intention of Divine Will, there would be no Consciousness and no cosmic Intelligence to create and uphold the appearance of creation, and even Nothingness could be not be. The Infinite Silence of pure Nothingness is due to the

Infinite Dynamism of pure Divinity. They have always been one wholeness.

There is no difference between pure Force and pure Silence, yet, remaining as One, pure Force reigns Supreme.

It appears that we have a real physical body and that the world and universe is filled with objects, phenomena, planets, stars and galaxies. But from the ultimate perspective, there is no such thing as a physical body or a separate world of matter, animate or inanimate. Everything is the one life of pure Divinity in appearance. All levels of energy and intelligence that appear as multifarious existence are the shapes, qualities and flows of the *supreme masking power* of pure Divinity.

This incredible illusory power of supreme Divinity has tricked, not only the conditioned mind into the belief and experience that the physical body and world is a solid physical reality, but it has also tricked the awakened mind. The unbounded pure Awareness of awakened Consciousness is also limited: firstly, by the experience that *everything is in my Self* in Cosmic Consciousness; and then, by the experience that *everything is my SELF* in Unity Consciousness. Any sense of Self, individual, cosmic or universal, is a product of the great illusory power of pure Divinity. Even pure Nothingness itself only knows its non-existence and is not, initially, in touch with its own Supreme Power that appears as all existence.

If the vehicle of perception (the nervous system) is not sufficiently refined, and the supreme power of pure Divinity is not yet directly experienced as everything everywhere, it is easy to get caught in the experience that the physical world is a solid reality, or caught in the attitude that the world is just an illusion. But when seen with refined perception in its total perspective, the world is found to be neither real nor unreal. It is not a reality, and it is not an illusion. It is the *Supreme Masking Power* of pure Divinity in appearance! When that reality is seen, there could not be anything more real, or as immeasurably beautiful, as this "illusory existence".

PURE DIVINITY—THE DIVINE MOTHER OF ALL

The wholeness of non-existence, and all manifest and un-manifest existence, pure Divinity is an unlimited field of the infinite power of Nothingness. Beyond all ideas of He, She or It, the power of pure Divinity is distinctly feminine in character. It is that supreme force that has given birth to everything, including the ability for Nothingness to know itself.

Pure Divinity is the original motivating force causing pure Consciousness to be conscious, pure Intelligence to be intelligent, and pure Existence to exist. It is She who inspires the creator to create, the maintainer to maintain, and the destroyer to destroy. She is the Divine Mother of all.

All the streams of universal Intelligence—conducting, and appearing as man, nature and all beings—owe their existence to Her. They flow in the infinite vortex of her limitless power as energies of her supreme Divinity, completely absorbed in their allotted duties, continuously spinning the web of world appearance. She is the vital energy force of all life energies and the intrinsic Divine Light in the light of pure Consciousness. Her breath is pure Being. Cosmic Intelligence is propelled by her thought force. The entire creation, Her Maya. As the sun radiates light, she radiates the appearance of creation.

By Her will the heart beats, the sun shines, the seasons change and the world turns. She orchestrates the movement of the planets, stars and galaxies. Spawning countless universes, overseeing their creation, maintenance, evolution and dissolution, she plays. The combined light emanating from all the suns and stars in the universe, is but a candle compared to the omnipresent light of pure Consciousness, which itself, completely dissolves in the face of Her Supreme Luminescence. Without her Light, there is neither light nor darkness. Without Her power, even the Nothingness is not.

She is the individual self, the cosmic Self and the universal SELF of everyone. She hides deep within the Nothingness as pure subtle intention, so that when Her Supreme light is finally revealed (through fully awakened Consciousness), She can revel in the sublime light and divine majesty of Her own unending supreme glory and grace in the guise of creation.

Pure Divinity is the cause, beginning, course and end. She is the essence and the image, the pure light and the expressed life. She is the source, guiding light, indweller and experiencer of all material, spiritual, and divine experience.

She is the Divine Presence that is permeating, pervading, animating and appearing as all the objects in the room and world around you, including that of your own body.

She is the timelessness in the present moment of Now, the purity in pure Awareness, the pure Aliveness in silent Presence, the pure knowing of universal Intellect.

She empowers all minds to think, all feelings to feel, all senses to perceive.

She is the power appearing as all Life.

Pure Divinity plays in the shades of light and darkness, positive and negative, divine and demonic, and yet remains far beyond it all.

Hidden deep within the Nothingness, yet found everywhere in the appearance of everything, there is nothing near or far, subtle or gross, micro or macro that is not Her. Everything seen and unseen is the reflection of Her pure Divine Light.

In Her, there is no you. There is only She experiencing Herself in the appearance of the world through the appearance of you.

She is the impulse of intention to Be in the hollow seed of pure Nothingness, causing Consciousness to sprout into the tree of creation and flower into world appearance, creation after creation throughout all eternity, *all the while remaining unmoved, unmodified, unchanged and uninvolved.* All existence is the Supreme luminescence of pure Divinity in appearance.

She is the Divine Mother of All.

...

O Divine Mother of all relative existence and absolute Being, You are immeasurably vast and supremely powerful.

Though beyond the knowing mind, being infinitely compassionate and omnipresent, some flavor of your Divinity can be felt in all hearts open and innocent.

Through this very act of seeing, reading, hearing, thinking and feeling, Your Supreme Divinity illumines Awareness itself, emanating a subtle sense of the pure essence of Your Divine Radiance through the surrounding Presence...

The fine flow of seeing, reading, knowing, feeling, draws You out of Your silent cave of Stillness, and out of Your guise as world appearance,

> *awakening Your remembrance in the heart of Being,*
>
> *awakening Your remembrance in all perception,*
>
> *infusing Divine Light into body, mind, heart and soul.*

Your Supreme Divinity is the source and cause of creation

> *every breath, Your Divine Will,*
>
> *giving life*
>
> *nourishing life*
>
> *flowing as pure Life itself*

You are the Supreme Force behind the life-force of Life,

> *the divine radiance appearing as creation*

the filament igniting the light of pure Awareness
the matrix and the substratum
the wholeness of the wholeness

Your Light is the eternal Sun of all spiritual light,
* radiating within the innermost core of all souls*
* the heart and soul of Universal Being*

You empower every being to think, feel, perceive and to Be
You are the cause of the seer,
the flow of the seeing and the appearance of the seen

You are the pure Light illumining the light of Consciousness

When vision is pure, the eyes see only You,
* dissolving in the proximity of Your Supreme Radiance,*
* surrendering to Your Supreme Luminosity,*
* the Seer, the Seeing and the Seen bow before you*
* in devotional surrender*

A flavor of your Divinity is felt in the surrounding Presence,
* in the space*
* in the air*
* in the light*
* in the objects of perception*
* in my body*

My body, mind, heart and soul feel your Divine Presence

My body is not "my" body. It is Your Body,

> *opening to its fullness through the image of me*

All bodies are Your Body in appearance. They are Your means of revealing the infinity of Your Supreme Divinity to Yourself

How can we be so foolish as to call You air, space, light, mind, body, world, universe, or even Supreme Self, when everything is but an appearance created by Your Supreme Power of Illusion? It has been Your pure Divine Light all along.

In You, there is no me, there is no SELF, there is no world, there is no universe,

> *there is only You in disguise*

Seeing through your apparel of world appearance, You shine brighter than millions of suns, radiating pure Divine Light, emanating supreme Glory and Grace...

You are the infinite abode of compassion and mercy,

> *the destroyer of fear*
>
> *the purveyor of Joy*
>
> *the fountainhead of Bliss*

You shine as the innocence in all things innocent and pure

You radiate the appearance of everything

Everything is beautiful when the eyes can see only You

You are the infinite abode of pure Love,
      the divine feeling felt in all hearts innocent and open.
The pure open-heart fills with divine joy,
      flowing in the infinite ocean of Your pure Supreme Love.

You are the fine feeling welling in the heart,
      penetrating deeply into the soul
      rising in devotion

You are pure Devotion,
      the fullness of heart
      the tidal wave of blissful Joy
      the teardrop shed in innocent surrender.

Radiating Divine Bliss in the innermost core of pure Being,
      Your Supreme Light shines,
      and all Life finds its eternal source and abode.

You are the ocean of Supreme Bliss,
      without beginning
      without end

There is only reverence, gratitude, devotion, surrender
      absorbed by Your Splendor, Glory and Grace

236

YOU are the only thing in this life that can truly be counted upon, for in time, everything held dear will eventually disappear, and this world and universe will be no more.

All life is dependent upon You and You alone

You are the only true refuge, the only safe harbor

There is nothing in this world, or in the infinity of worlds beyond, that is more precious

I surrender to You

There is only pure Surrender

There is only YOU...

...

Even if your feelings were not stirred while reading this, rest assured that the clear experience of pure Divinity is not just a mood, attitude, feeling or belief. It is a direct experience. It is only due to the absence of direct experience that belief is born. Beyond all moods, beliefs, imaginations, and beyond all existence, pure Divinity is the only thing that can truly be said to be Real.

In the state of Cosmic Consciousness, everything is *in* my Self. In Unity Consciousness, everything everywhere *is* my SELF. In Beyond Consciousness, everything is pure non-existence in appearance. In pure Divinity Consciousness, everything is pure Divinity in appearance. The world remains the same, only it is experienced with a clearer perception from a broader perspective in each state.

You may think you are just a human being, but the essence and ultimate reality of every atom and cell in your body, every thought in your mind, every feeling, sensation, perception and experience, is ultimately, pure Supreme Divinity. Pure Divinity is the cause and essence of Consciousness out of which the appearance of the universe, and the awareness of it, are composed.

REFINED DIVINE PERCEPTION

As in every state of Consciousness, the clarity of perception continues to refine and deepen; only from this perspective, all experience is in terms of pure Divinity. The world remains the same, but the direct experience is that everything is pure Divinity in appearance; and through the process of experiencing, pure Divinity continues to reveal more of its divine reality to itself.

There is no individual person, cosmic SELF, Being, Consciousness, Cosmic Intelligence, quantum field, subtle levels, world, or universe from this perspective. There is no perceiver, process of perceiving or perceived. There is only pure Divinity in the appearance of all of that, delighting in the finer revelations of Her own supreme radiance within and beyond the experience of life and activity of living.

Ordinary perception perceives only the objects and phenomena of experience. Refined Perception reveals the fine flows of the process of experiencing within all experience, which are the subtle levels, qualities and functions of Cosmic Intelligence perpetually creating the appearance of the objects and phenomena of experience. Still finer Perception reveals the finest impulses within the silence of pure Being that are propelling and directing the flows of Cosmic Intelligence that give rise to experience.

Beyond that, deep within the Nothingness, prior to Consciousness, rests the fundamental matrix of pure Supreme Divinity. The ultimate framework behind infinite Nothingness, Consciousness, Intelligence, creation, and all spiritual light, is exposed. It is the original, supreme power generator that initiates Consciousness and drives the universal forces of cosmic divine Intelligence to create, maintain and appear as creation. Shedding its apparel of world appearance, totally absorbed in its own supreme luminescence, pure Divinity reveals to itself its true unborn formless form and sublime eternal ethereal composition.

Appearing as if composed of countless crystal-like power centers, each radiating Supreme Divine Light, hidden by its own wholeness of peerless radiant Divine Light, the lattice of pure Divinity opens to perception. Each power center is a wholeness within itself, consisting of countless power centers superimposed one within the other ad infinitum. These vibrant pulsations, of concentrated pure light-energy-power centers of sheer Divine Bliss, perpetually radiate one uniform wholeness of sublime spiritual light—an eternal, beginning-less, endless ocean of pure Supreme Divinity.

Each power center radiates an irresistible, indestructible, all-powerful force of supreme Divine Light, while simultaneously continuously absorbing its own pure radiation. This creates an all-embracing, invincible wholeness, completely self-sufficient and self-sustaining—an infinitely silent and infinitely dynamic power generator of pure potentiality, permanently reverberating and resounding within itself in unceasing constant ecstatic divine surrender. Perpetually emitting and reabsorbing its own streams of radiant divine light, pure Divinity hides in the silence of its Nothingness as the supreme power of illusion, disguised in the appearance of creation.

Consciousness, universal Intelligence, and all levels of the apparent manifest and unmanifest creation (from the subtle spiritual levels, to the activity of the quantum realms, to the motions of the cosmos) are the effect of this eternal pulsation of supreme Divinity. Unseen by the mind and senses, it is the activity of the supreme reality of your life.

The physical body is only the surface appearance of the grand wholeness of your total Being. Deep within your own body/mind are the subtler realms of your existence—the prana and cosmic energies, the chakras, and all the subtle and causal levels of existence. The universe itself is the apparent manifest expression of these subtle cosmic realities of your own body. Beyond all that is this supreme power matrix of pure Divinity; it is the true essence and ultimate substance of the human form and all perceptions.

The quintessence of all bodies and all levels of manifest and unmanifest existence is the body of pure Divinity. Birth, growth, death, decay and regeneration are due to the ultimate power of illusion of pure Divinity in its perpetual surrender within itself, continuously revealing more and more of Its infinite, inexhaustible Supreme nature to itself.

These forces of pure power and surrender, compelling Consciousness and its universal Intelligence to appear as individual, collective and cosmic life, continue to open more clearly to perception. Though the full magnitude and force of this supreme light-power dynamic cannot manifest fully through any form in this age, the time is fast approaching when, at least some flavor of that rising pure Divine essence, will influence the minds, hearts and souls of everyone.

It is clear from this perspective that there is no such thing as an objective physical reality, or an individual ego sense, mind or personality. There is no "you" experiencing the Divine. There is only pure Divinity experiencing itself through the appearance of you and your perceptions. The quantum field flows of universal Intelligence that create the appearance of your body and its perceptions of the world are driven by impulses of pure Divinity. Universal Intelligence and Consciousness itself, are ultimately the product of the surrender of pure Divinity to its own Supreme Light.

Our physical bodies are the product of the notions of the conditioned mind created by unfulfilled desires, impressions and resultant karmas due to attachment and false identification with physical appearance. The subtle light body and causal body are the product of the intention of universal mind. But the true essence of all bodies, gross and subtle, is the one absolute uncreated eternal body of Supreme Divinity—the body of pure Divine Surrender. This body of pure Divinity has been glimpsed by the great sages, holy rishis and perfected beings throughout time.

We are all expressions of this same one eternal absolute pure Divinity body that has been forgotten for millennia in the appearance of the many. We have been so lost in endless streams of desire, that lifetime after lifetime has been spent chasing after physical, spiritual or divine phenomena, and the true absolute Supreme reality of life has been missed. Every desire of the mind is ultimately a desire of the Supreme to return home to the fullness of Itself through the appearance of you.

A measure of the degree of the holistic unfoldment of the fullness of Consciousness is the ever-increasing degree of innocent, pure devotion felt in the mind, heart and soul. Pure Devotion is unconditioned, innocent divine surrender from the level of pure Being, free from attachment to any person, object or phenomena. It is the fragrance issuing from pure Divinity. It is the product of holistic integration and refinement, and an indication of the degree to which pure Divinity has revealed itself at that point of experience.

If you pray for anything in life, pray for the capacity to experience pure Devotion, for it is the flint that sparks the flame of pure Truth that opens the mind, heart and soul to surrender to the supreme light of pure Divinity. When devotion is sincere and pure, it is impossible for pure Divinity to resist, for it is through the innocent surrender of a pure open heart that She can reveal more of Her own supreme Divinity to Herself.

Awakening to the total reality of being Consciousness is a beautiful thing, but awakening to the pure Divinity that is the ultimate cause of Consciousness itself, is quite another. It is beyond words like awakening and enlightenment. Pure Divinity is the sovereign power and omnipotent force of supreme radiant Divine Light that is the ultimate cause of all Awakenings. There is no end to the infinity of perfection and bliss in that supreme Divine Light.

≈≈≈

CHAPTER FIFTEEN

TOTAL VISION

Summary and Conclusion

YOU ARE CONSCIOUSNESS

It may be difficult to believe everything you have read so far, but as you continue your spiritual journey into reality, you will gradually open to this truth for yourself. There is so much more to life than we have been living. We've been asleep to the profundity of what life is. Our senses perceive only a small fraction of the known reality, and our brains only use a small portion of their potential, and yet, with this limited sensory and mental capacity, somehow, we still think that what we experience is reality.

In truth, nothing is as it appears. The so-called "real physical world" of matter is made of energy vortex-like points of unbounded quantum fields of infinite possibility that are not at all physical. The world is not a separate physical reality out there somewhere on its own independent of Consciousness. Our perceptions of the world around us, including our own bodies, are created by, and only exist because of conscious Awareness. Without Consciousness, nothing could possibly exist anywhere for anyone.

Awareness itself is the simple sense of Being, the sense that "I Am". Everyone experiences that sense of existing, of simply being.

It is on this level of the pure sense of Being that we are all connected as one. It is universal Being. On its own level, not associated with thoughts, feelings and perceptions, the universal sense of Being is the timeless eternal present moment of Now—an unbounded field of pure Awareness.

Pure Awareness, fully awake to itself, is pure Consciousness. Pure Consciousness is the experiencer, the process of experiencing and the object of its own experience. Individual consciousness *is* unbounded pure Consciousness that has become temporarily falsely identified with the individual mind/body and its perceptions.

We have gone through life conditioned by our perceptions and experiences, unawake to the true universal reality of our existence. We have been caught in the field of experience, lost to the real *experiencer* and the underlying mechanics of *experiencing*—lost to the true reality of our SELF. If we are not experiencing the true reality of our SELF, as the real experiencer and the underlying mechanics of experiencing, how can our experience possibly be real or complete?

Our ordinary experience of the world is "I am the experiencer, and the world out there is separate from me". Careful introspection reveals that the real experiencer is not the person aware of the world, but rather, it is the *Awareness* that is aware of the person who is aware of the world. This Awareness is the pure sense of Being and existing. It is your real Self. It is Consciousness itself.

Being the experiencer, the process of experiencing and the experience of itself, Consciousness has a three-fold structure. As the *Experiencer* of itself, Consciousness is pure Awareness—the true universal sense of Being and existing experienced by everyone. It is the same field of wakeful Awareness in which your mind, body and all your perceptions exist right now. Your personal sense of being and existing *is* universal pure Being falsely identified with the individual mind, body and perceptions. It is the same universal one Self of all, and the underlying fundamental reality of everything.

In the *Process of Experiencing* itself, Consciousness is pure Intelligence. All the qualities, traits and functions of your individual mind and body are universal qualities of Intelligence that are naturally inherent in Consciousness. The activity of your body functioning, your mind thinking, your emotions feeling and your senses perceiving the world around you *is* the activity of universal Intelligence. That universal Intelligence is the finest cosmic level of your mind and it is responsible for creating and sustaining the appearance of the world and universe.

In its perpetual *Experience* of itself, Consciousness appears as the objects and phenomena of perception. Your perceptions of the world are flows of Consciousness in its perpetual experience of itself, molded into concrete appearance by the universal Intelligence inherent at every point within it. Perceptions are thought forms, created and displayed on the unbounded field of pure Awareness by the universal Intelligence at the finest level of your mind.

All levels of Intelligence that form the fundamental constituents of the universe and laws of creation are naturally inherent in Consciousness. These same levels of Intelligence are the subtle levels of your own nervous system. The quantum level of your brain is a boundless universal field of pure Intelligence, continuously creating the appearance of objectivity and orchestrating all life experience. It is a lively field of infinite potentiality—the universal extension of your own mind. This unconscious universal aspect of your mind is the same fundamental quantum field level of the universe that has been glimpsed by physics.

The quantum field level of life is an expression of the flow of infinite Intelligence inherent in Consciousness. It is an aspect of the inner reality of your existence and the boundless extension of your total Being, and this can be opened to direct experience. The person you call "me" is the manifest expression of a point of that quantum field level of infinite Intelligence that has become falsely identified with the body/mind and the objects of its own creation.

Your individual self *is* universal Self falsely identified with the mind. Your individual mind *is* universal Mind functioning at a point of individual appearance. Your entire personhood *is* universal Intelligence in individual appearance. The world and universe are the expressed appearance of the universal quantum field reality of your own brain and nervous system. The subtlest universal reality of your own total being is the DNA of the universe. You *are* infinite Consciousness temporarily identified with individual experience.

Due to repetitive experience, Consciousness became conditioned and identified (with the appearance of objects and phenomena created in its process of knowing itself) and became lost to its true unbounded universal reality. This false identification created an apparent subject/object division in the field of unbounded pure Consciousness, where there is, in reality, only oneness. From this incomplete perspective, the mind and body appear as individual, and the world appears to be a separate objective reality.

However, the objects and phenomena of the body, world and universe have never been real physical material objects of experience separate from the consciousness of the experiencer. Perceptions have always been created in the brain by your own consciousness. Objects appearing in conscious awareness are made by Consciousness. The world around you (including your own body) is created by Consciousness in its process of being conscious of itself, and is nothing but Consciousness in appearance.

Consciousness is all there is.

WAKING FROM THE DREAM

In a dream, your mind can create anything, and you can be anyone. A whole lifetime of experiences can pass by, and suddenly you wake up and realize you have only been dreaming. What happened to time in that dream? What happened to the world you experienced in that dream? Who were the people? Who were you? It all seemed very real, but it was only a dream created by your mind. All the people, situations, events, time and place in your dream world were all created by your own consciousness.

Similarly, when you awaken from this present waking state experience to who you really are, you find it is very much like waking from a dream. You discover that you are the Awareness that is aware of the person. As Awareness itself, you are unbounded silence, peace and freedom—separate from, and unaffected by what is happening in the mind, body or life experience. You discover that you, as Awareness itself, are the same pure Awareness and universal sense of existence that everyone experiences. There is only one field of pure Awareness, one Self. Everything exists in and due to that field of pure Awareness. Refined Perception in this state opens the awareness to the organizing intelligence orchestrating the life of the universe.

As the awakening deepens, another shift in perspective occurs. The unbounded pure Awareness awakens to itself as being all objects and phenomena of perception. Everything is directly experienced as being my SELF. "I am everything everywhere. Everything is Consciousness, and I am Consciousness. Consciousness is all there is". Refined perception in this perspective reveals that the flow of Consciousness experiencing itself is the organizing intelligence responsible for creating and orchestrating the appearance of the universe.

A clearer awakening takes place when Consciousness transcends this universal sense of Being. The boundless SELF disappears, and along with it, all existence disappears. Everything is experienced as being non-existent, uncreated pure Nothingness. Further refinement of perception within this perspective reveals a still more subtle causal level of divine power hidden deep within the Nothingness, prior to Consciousness and its qualities of cosmic creative intelligence.

When the perception of this Divine Power reaches a critical level of intensity and clarity in that state, another shift in perspective and perception occurs. The ultimate power source and cause of all causes, material, spiritual and divine, opens to experience as being the pure radiant light of Supreme Divinity. That supreme luminosity has been disguised in the appearance of the universe and creation all along. Everything is found to be that. Pure Divinity is all there is, and all there has ever been.

The full cycle of Consciousness knowing itself at the point of human experience is complete, and can now begin to unfold and deepen through the experience of living. The universal divine reality of the body continues to open more clearly to perception and is lived through individual experience on the surface appearance of life.

These awakenings are unmistakable and are the same for everyone. Once clearly experienced and fully integrated, they are never lost. They cannot be missed because the perspective in each state is 180 degrees from the previous, even though it remains the same one unbounded field of pure Awareness. Each state is a progressive unfoldment of awakening to the fullness of its total Divine reality.

UNIVERSAL PERCEPTION

In unawakened consciousness, the unbounded reality of the Self and the universal field of Intelligence responsible for perception and experience are not experienced. As a result, the true reality of life is not fully experienced. Everyone sees from their own individual perspective based on the clarity or dullness of their consciousness. From one perspective, perception and understanding seem to be correct, but from a broader perspective, the exact opposite may be true. (Paradigm shifts in worldview, such as the earth being flat and the sun revolving around the earth, are obvious examples of this.)

Though the content of thought, feeling, perception and action appears to be individual, the underlying forces initiating all thought and action are cosmic and universal. For perception and understanding to be accurate and true, and for action to be completely life-supporting, it is necessary, not only to be permanently established in the absolute unbounded reality of pure Being, but also, to have a clear refined perception of the universal qualities of Intelligence responsible for all thought and action.

Every quality and function of the mind, body and personality is a frequency of quantum field universal Intelligence functioning through the point of individual appearance. Some of these universal frequencies are expansive and progressive, while some are restrictive and limiting. Within pure Consciousness itself, these universal frequencies are in perfect balance. But due to the false identification with the individual mind/body, imbalance is inevitably created. Perception, experience and reality become narrowed by individual experience, out of sync with the natural flow of universal Intelligence, and life becomes a struggle. All problems, conflict and suffering in individual and collective life are ultimately due to thought and action out of tune with the natural flow of universal Intelligence.

After clear Awakening, as perception refines, universal Intelligence begins to function more freely through individual appearance, and the forces governing individual and collective life can be more clearly perceived. When perception is clear, instead of seeing individual separate people, what is also perceived are the universal qualities of Intelligence acting through individuals, groups, organizations, communities, cities, states, countries, world and the universe. Ultimately, there are *only* universal qualities of Intelligence functioning in the appearance of individual life. These qualities of universal Intelligence have been governing individual and collective consciousness all along.

Despite what appears to be happening in the world from the perspective of media or popular opinion, there is something far more powerful and profound going on in the subtle realms of consciousness. Due to the many Awakenings taking place in the world, the imbalance in life created by false identification with individual appearance is gradually shifting.

The balance of life is in the process of being restored.

The qualities of intelligence responsible for contraction resulting in narrow thinking and limited vision, which have been dominantly controlling individual and collective life, are gradually losing their grip. Consciousness is expanding. More positive, expansive qualities are beginning to take their rightful place on the surface of life. The world is going through a paradigm shift at the most fundamental level.

THE AWAKENING WORLD

People all over the world today are spontaneously awakening to the unbounded reality of their true Self, and a deeper experience of the true divine reality of life is beginning to unfold. We are on the cusp of a new age of Enlightenment so far beyond the imagination, that even a hint of it, as conveyed through the pages of this book, would be labeled a dream, fantasy or delusion by most people. But, it is the natural progression that occurs due to the awakening to reality as it really is, uncolored by the conditioning and impressions of objective physical appearance. It is the restricted life we have been living, falsely identified with the objects of appearance, devoid of the experience of our real Self and true divine nature, that is the dream, fantasy and delusion.

We are now living in an age where consciousness, know-ledge and creativity are rapidly expanding. This is a good thing, but as consciousness expands, the mind's concepts also expand. Without clear Awakening and the necessary refine-ment of perception, understanding and vision cannot be com-pletely holistic, and in some cases may even be damaging to life. Partial knowledge can be a dangerous thing.

When the universal reality of individual life is missing in the consciousness of society, shallow separate limited individual-istic viewpoints are still prevalent. It is still an age where the knowledge, understanding and experience of enlightenment by the vast majority of the population is incomplete, distorted or non-existent. Many who have already awakened still have only a partial grasp of what full enlightenment really means.

On the surface, it may appear as though the world is in per-il, or perhaps even sliding backwards. The forces of ignorance, limiting higher awareness, that have been dominating life are feeling threatened by the fast pace of change caused by the rise of consciousness. The separate little ego/mind is fighting to defend its hold and control over individual and collective life. But, at a finer level, the higher qualities of unity, harmony, purity, love, compassion, kindness and goodness, are gradually gaining strength in the collective consciousness. Yet, these beautiful qualities are still fragile, vulnerable and subject to change without the permanent stability of clear Awakening. The need for complete knowledge and experience of the full range of Consciousness, in society today, could not be greater.

In the state of refined Unity Consciousness and beyond, the true unity of life can finally be lived, and it is unshakable. Con-sciousness is no longer overshadowed by objective appear-ance. Everything is experienced as my SELF. It is the beginning of living a completely balanced state of life. The deeply-rooted impressions and stresses, that have limited Consciousness to objective experience, have been released to a great degree, and the divine reality of life begins to unfold without much restriction. The natural unity of life is spontaneously lived through all thoughts, feelings, perceptions and actions.

With refined perception in this state, the cosmic Intelligence, that has always been functioning through individual appearance, opens to Awareness. Life is lived more naturally in accord with nature's intelligence. The higher qualities of universal Intelligence function more easily through individual appearance, and life is lived in increasing joy and fullness, as it was naturally intended.

Imagine a world where peace, freedom, joy, lightness, clear perception, harmony, beauty, love and compassion are dominant in the consciousness of everyone. Imagine a world where arrogance, pride, envy, jealousy, selfishness, lust, anger, hate and fear are greatly diminished. It would be a world of peace, abundance, happiness and fulfilment, unlike anything we have ever known. It would literally be a "heaven on earth".

This transformation is in the process of happening right now.

The true essential foundation and fabric of life itself is rising within the minds, hearts and souls of everyone. Consciousness is in the process of Awakening to its true Divine reality. The entire life of the world is being transformed from an age of ignorance to an Age of Enlightenment.

Deep within the boundless reality of your Being, at the finest universal level of your mind, there is an infinite field of pure divine energy and intelligence. It is the true nature of your SELF. It is from this level that the universal Intelligence at the quantum field level of your brain is creating and maintaining the appearance of the world around you. When Awareness opens to this level, the individual mind spontaneously begins to function more in accord with the laws of nature that conduct the universe. Those who function from this level have the power to influence the consciousness of society in a positive, holistic way, and to create a beneficial, nourishing and evolutionary effect on all levels of life.

AWAKENING THE WORLD

Just one person functioning more in tune with nature's intelligence has a beneficial effect on the surroundings. Large groups of people meditating and practicing specific techniques that enliven that field of universal Intelligence have been shown to create a positive effect on society.[1] The knowledge of the group dynamics of Consciousness gives us a practical means to help create a balancing effect on the collective consciousness of the world. There are many groups and communities around the world that are creating a positive effect on society. But the range of their influence is limited by their numbers, the effectiveness and duration of their practice, and the level of consciousness from which the practices are done.

After awakening to refined Unity Consciousness (and beyond), the beneficial effect of group practice on the consciousness of society is far more pronounced and profound. Consciousness not only knows itself fully, but it is awake to the field of infinite potentiality and the finest levels of universal Intelligence from where nature functions. The enlivenment of that universal level of life has a powerful, life-supporting influence on consciousness everywhere.

Every human is, knowingly or unknowingly, an instrument of the Divine, but due to the impressions and stresses accumulated from the false identification with the mind/body, the vast majority of people are not awake to this reality. At some point,

---

[1] Large group practice of advanced siddhi techniques can have a beneficial effect on the life of society, reducing conflict, crime, accident and sickness rates. Collected Papers—Volumes 1—6 http://maharishi-programmes.globalgoodnews.com/maharishi-effect/research.html

perhaps after many years of living in the awakened state, the realization dawns: *the only means pure Divinity has to experience the fullness and fine details of itself, in the appearance of the world and universe, is through fully awakened human Consciousness.*

Because there is only one Consciousness, the effect of the enlightened who have opened to the field of pure Divinity naturally enlivens the divine evolutionary qualities of intelligence in the consciousness of society. As such, it is in the hands of the fully enlightened to ensure the positive direction of the consciousness of society and the world.

The enlightened, who are functioning from that universal field of infinite potentiality, on a subtle level, have been upholding the evolutionary direction of society all along. However, with the application of the knowledge of the group dynamics of consciousness, the effect could be greatly enhanced. Pure Divinity is experienced more deeply through groups of clearly awakened people. The more clearly pure Divinity is experienced, the more it is enlivened in the collective consciousness of society.

Imagine groups of fully enlightened people in refined Unity Consciousness (and beyond) all around the world, positively influencing the collective consciousness. What a world that would be! Even one group, functioning from that level of universal mind, would help guide world consciousness in the direction of greater peace, harmony and unity at a rapid pace. Even groups of people moving in this direction are of enormous benefit to society. In this age, with the world so divided and disharmonious, the time is ripe for unifying groups of this nature to be formed.

The Awakening World Society Foundation (AWSF), a nonprofit organization, has been established for this purpose.

The world is awakening. Everyone is a de-facto member of the Awakening World Society by just being alive in this age.

The true foundation of this awakening is the pure Divine Power behind Consciousness itself.

The AWSF has been formed to share the knowledge and experience of the full range of Consciousness and to help create groups of awakened people. Its administration is on the level of the universal field of Intelligence that is conducting the universe, enlivened by those around the world who have awakened to the unbounded reality of their true Being.

The AWSF provides a clear expression of the fundamental essence of universal truth that lies at the basis of all ideologies, philosophies, religions and sciences. It embraces all traditions of knowledge that have sound, time-tested, scientifically validated programs and techniques for the holistic unfoldment of life in the direction of greater perfection and total enlightenment.

It is a call to the awakened to join together to enliven the universal field of Consciousness for the benefit of life everywhere. With the knowledge of the full range of Consciousness, and with the clear, direct experience of the universal reality of total Being, a lasting state of peace, unity and harmony is not only possible, it is inevitable.

TOTAL PERSPECTIVE

Within the infinite vastness of Nothingness, prior to creation, there is a latent unmanifest seed of pure intention to know and to Be. This seed of pure intention is the spark that ignites the light of pure Consciousness. Driven by the power of this initial intention, Consciousness continually curves back upon itself to experience its own infinite reality. This perpetual motion creates discrete frequencies of knowing (waves of universal Intelligence) within the infinite ocean of Consciousness. This flow of Intelligence is the universal aspect of your own mind and quantum field reality of your brain. Everything in the universe is the appearance generated by these flows of universal Intelligence.

Without that initial impulse to Be, there would be no Consciousness, no Intelligence, no existence, no person, no world or universe, and even the vast Nothingness would not know itself. That initial intention is the *Pure Power of Supreme Divinity*—the power that pervades, permeates and appears as all existence. The expression of that subtle intention on the surface appearance of life, at a point, is the human body/mind. All levels of creation, and all form and phenomena, are the expressed appearance of its infinity. Everything is made of infinite pure Consciousness which, at its core, is pure Divinity. The essential constituent and foundation of all existence, has been pure Divinity all along.

It is that supreme power of Pure Divinity that has given birth to Consciousness and its streams of Intelligence that create the appearance of all bodies, worlds and universes. It is ever in the act of molding, protecting, balancing and nourishing all creation so that life can mature to its infinite divine reality and perfection. There is no end to the unfoldment of perfection, as pure Divinity itself is infinite, eternal, unlimited, without beginning or end.

This reality unfolds to direct perception as Consciousness awakens to the fullness of its internal dynamics, and then transcends its own unbounded universal sense of Being. Consciousness expands to encompass the full range of its existence and non-existence—and it is all Divine.

From this perspective, there is no such thing as a separate individual person. Individuality is found to be universal Intelligence functioning at the point of individual appearance. The separate world "out there" is found to be universal Intelligence in the appearance of form and phenomena. As atoms and subatomic particles are now known to be the epiphenomena of universal quantum fields, individual physical life is experienced by the enlightened to be the epiphenomena of the flows of universal Intelligence activated in the process of Consciousness being conscious of itself, driven by the power of pure Divinity.

The world remains the same, only life is experienced as the flow of the internal dynamics of the Divine. The divine qualities of Intelligence—the laws of nature that structure the appearance of creation, *are* the quantum field expressions of the universal qualities of your own personhood. The individual body/mind is a configuration of all the qualities of universal Intelligence functioning together at the point of individual appearance. The reality of the cosmic body is lived in the appearance of individual human form.

The physical universe is the appearance created by the play of the light of Divine Consciousness—the qualities and flavors of the flow of its own wholeness of pure Divinity. Divine Intelligence has been creating, guiding, and conducting the appearance of life all along.

Like fish swimming in the ocean searching for water to drink, we have been living and breathing pure Divinity, completely oblivious to the true reality of our existence. We have been living in the "heaven on earth" that we've always dreamt of, only our consciousness and perception have not sufficiently opened to experience it! Everything is "made in heaven" out of the material of pure Divinity. Not only have we managed to create a gross physical world out of the fabric of pure Divinity, but many of us have managed to create a hell on earth out of it.

At some point, you will wake up to discover that you are no longer an individual person walking through physical space, breathing physical air, seeing physical light, and living in a physical world. You will find that it has all been pure Divinity in appearance all along. Once that reality is clearly experienced, it is never lost. You can only see reality as it really is from the broadest possible perspective. The universe is the radiance of the divine majesty of pure Supreme Divinity in appearance. Far beyond the knowing of the mind, intellect, senses and emotions, it is revealed of its own accord in the innermost core of the boundless SELF as its own pure essence.

THE ULTIMATE REALITY

You are not a human being searching for the divine. You are Consciousness in the process of awakening to your fullness as boundless pure Divinity. The human being is the expressed appearance of the total internal dynamics of Consciousness knowing itself at a point, and the means for Consciousness to reveal its own supreme reality to itself. Evolution is the gradual unfoldment of Consciousness to its total Divine reality through the appearance of form.

The ultimate reality of clear enlightened seeing is:

There is only Pure Divinity. Everything has been Pure Divinity in appearance all along!

You are Pure Divinity itself, still in the process of remembering the fullness of itself through the mechanism of human appearance. You are not just a child of God—*you are God*, but still in embryo. Your mind/body is created out of pure Divinity, and is the vehicle Consciousness uses to awaken to that supreme reality.

Of all the billions of species in this world and beyond, to be born a human being is the greatest blessing of all. Our time on earth is precious and should not be wasted in trivial pursuit. Every moment, every breath, is a blessing to be cherished. Now is the time to put attention on true enlightenment and not get so caught in lesser goals that only deflect from the real purpose of your existence. There are so many interesting spiritual concepts, philosophies and experiences that entice the curious seeking mind, but they may only lead to further phenomena, beliefs, partial understanding and limited experience—not to the goal.

Though many spiritual movements and religions were originally inspired by an enlightened teacher, over time, the direct experience is lost and pure truth falls into concepts, beliefs, rituals and imaginations of the unenlightened mind. The spiritual world of phenomena and the physical world of matter are the products of the unawakened mind, unconscious of the pure Divinity out of which everything is ultimately composed.

All the great enlightened saints, sages and seers throughout time, even though worthy of reverence themselves, surrender to that divine effulgence of the Supreme Divine power source that resides within, yet beyond, the appearance of everything.

Living in freedom and joy, fully awake to the total divine reality of life, is your birthright. It is the one reality of life to which everyone eventually awakens when the mind finally surrenders and the search ends. There is only one unbounded infinite totality, so divine in its nature that the mirage of creation completely vanishes in the pure radiance of its supreme illumination. It is pure Divine majesty beyond all measure and comparison.

This is the direct, unmistakable, unshakable experience of reality as it is in the fully awakened state. At some point in this life, or in the next, you will awaken to this reality, and it will be undeniable. All your beliefs, concepts and experiences up to that point will completely vanish in the face of that radiant Divine Light.

DIVINE JOY

Your real Being is unbounded pure Divine Joy. Some degree of pure joy, peace, freedom and fullness has always been with you. It is the most intimate part of you, beyond all thought and emotion, underlying and pervading all your perceptions within the silent depth of your soul. It is the finest innermost core of omnipresent pure Being.

It is everywhere in the alive Presence all around you right now...

It is within the clear, silent, wakeful Awareness that is enabling your mind to think, and your eyes to see these words and the world around you.

The natural, effortless flow of the senses perceiving, the feelings feeling, and the mind thinking is the manifest expression of the perpetual flow of the silent joy of absolute pure Being. When that flow is felt in simple, innocent purity, it is the flow of pure Divine joy. It is the eternal flow of infinite Consciousness ceaselessly opening to its Divine wholeness, fullness and sublime light.

When you innocently favor the boundless sense of quiet peace and joy within you, that is what will become more dominant in your life. That inner spark of freedom, lightness and joy will continue to brighten, until one day, it will ignite into the pure light and Divine joy of fully illumined Consciousness. When you favor the drama of the mind and life experience, that is what will continue to dominate, and the real purpose of life itself will be lost.

What you have been seeking is not found in material success, possessions, power, knowledge, loving relationships, or anything else in this illusory world. As charming as that may be, it is only temporary. It will constantly change throughout life and eventually disappear altogether.

The only measure of a truly successful life is the ever-increasing degree of pure divine joy and fullness of Being that becomes indelibly infused into the nature of the body, mind, heart and soul throughout the course of your life. The direct experience of being that all-pervading boundless supreme Divine Joy is the true goal and ultimate purpose of life. All material and spiritual goals are insignificant compared to that.

Have your goals and desires, they are all a part of life, but be innocently awake to the inner peace, silence and joy that is here right now, underlying all streams of desire. The fulfilment of all relative goals will eventually leave you feeling shallow and unfulfilled if the absolute pure Joy of your inner Being has not been awakened. The boundless divine joy and fullness of Being is the only thing that can bring satisfaction to the wavering mind because that is the true nature of your Self. It is the only thing that is real and ever-lasting, and the only thing you will take with you when the body is gone.

Rather than favoring the drama of mind and emotions, fall back to that underlying inner sense of simple innocent, pure joy, peace and freedom. It is always present in the innermost core of your being and in the Presence around you.

Innocently be with the Stillness and Alive Presence within and all around you right now...

Remember that Stillness and Presence whenever you get overshadowed by thoughts, emotions, and circumstances. At some point, when the time is right, in That you will remain.

Eventually, you will discover that there is only pure Divinity—infinite, absolute, boundless and eternal—the ultimate essence, source, cause, and creator of the universe of You. Into that ocean of pure Truth, Fullness and Divine Joy, you are destined to merge.

This is Enlightenment. It is so profound. It is the real purpose of life and the only thing that is truly worthwhile. Go for the highest. It is the easiest to attain because it is what you already are, and it is the only thing that is real.

ENDLESS BEGINNING

If you have been reading this book from the beginning, you have had a taste of a reality far beyond the wildest imagination of the general population, which, at this point in time, is only experienced by a rare few. You have had a glimpse into the Incredible Reality of You.

This insight and budding experience into the innermost depth of your Being will not be easily forgotten. If you have been innocent and open while reading this, like a seed, it will germinate in the fertile soil of your inner being. At some point, it will sprout into true wisdom that will blossom into profound realization and undeniable experience that will cut asunder all previous beliefs, concepts, experiences and perceptions ever held by the mind.

You have unknowingly stepped foot into the quicksand of pure Truth so profound that you will never again be able to step out. From now on, each step you take forward or back in life will take you deeper. Even though your mind may not realize it, the infinite Divine Intelligence within the innermost core of your being has been stirred. It has begun its journey home. It will continue to pull you deeper and deeper into pure Being, and it will not stop until you reach the true Divine reality of all existence—and there is absolutely nothing you can do about it.

So just sit back, relax, let go, and enjoy...

You hold in your hands a key to the unfoldment of the most profound and far-reaching knowledge of the total reality of life known to humankind. When you get bogged down in the mundane existence of life, read and reread these pages to remind yourself of what life is really about, and to hasten your pace of awakening to *the Incredible Reality of You.*

THE BEGINNING.

ACKNOWLEDGEMENTS

With deep gratitude to the wisdom of the Vedic Masters of the Holy Tradition, most recently embodied in the forms of Brahmananda Saraswati and Maharishi Mahesh Yogi, and to all the enlightened teachers in the past, present and future.

With gratitude, and deep love, to my beautiful wife and partner Lucia, who herself is a great embodiment of knowledge, wisdom, righteousness, truth, purity and divinity.

A special thank you to Jeanette and John for editing and proof-reading. Thank you to Scott, Richard, Monique and David for your comments and suggestions.

ABOUT THE AUTHOR

LUCIALORN (Lucia and Lawrence [lorn] Hoff) are contemporary spiritual teachers from Canada with over 45 years of experience in meditation and yoga. They have both had profound spontaneous spiritual awakenings and share their knowledge and experience through books, retreats, audio, video, and live webcasts.

The Incredible Reality of You arises from the stages and states of awakened Consciousness they have experienced. These states of Consciousness are universal and have been experienced and recorded by enlightened seers throughout time. Lorn and Lucia are not part of any religion or spiritual organization. Their teaching is based on the simple universal truths found in the silent pure Awareness of the consciousness of everyone.

They are the founders of The Awakening World Society Foundation, a non-profit organization for the advancement of the knowledge and experience of awakened Consciousness. They reside on Vancouver Island, BC in Canada.

www.lucialorn.net

The Awakening World Society Foundation

Awakening World Publishing

PO 373 Chemainus, BC

Canada V0R 1K0

WWW.AWAKENINGWORLD.NET

Ingram Content Group UK Ltd.
Milton Keynes UK
UKHW040708030423
419530UK00001B/21